AF904482

# Anxiety and Related Disorders Interview Schedule for DSM-5® (ADIS-5L)

*Lifetime Version*

## Client Interview Schedule

Timothy A. Brown
David H. Barlow

OXFORD
UNIVERSITY PRESS

OXFORD
UNIVERSITY PRESS

Oxford University Press is a department of the University of Oxford. It furthers the University's objective of excellence in research, scholarship, and education by publishing worldwide.

Oxford New York
Auckland Cape Town Dar es Salaam Hong Kong Karachi
Kuala Lumpur Madrid Melbourne Mexico City Nairobi
New Delhi Shanghai Taipei Toronto

With offices in
Argentina Austria Brazil Chile Czech Republic France Greece
Guatemala Hungary Italy Japan Poland Portugal Singapore
South Korea Switzerland Thailand Turkey Ukraine Vietnam



Published in the United States of America by
Oxford University Press
198 Madison Avenue, New York, NY 10016



ISBN 978–0–19–932477–4

9 8 7 6 5

Printed in the United States of America
on acid-free paper

## ABOUT THE AUTHORS

**Timothy A. Brown** received his PsyD from the Virginia Consortium for Professional Psychology in 1988. He has published numerous scientific articles and chapters in the area of anxiety and mood disorders, and quantitative research methods. Presently, he is Professor in the Psychology Department at Boston University, and Director of Research and Research Administration of the Center for Anxiety and Related Disorders at Boston University. In addition to his own funded research on the classification and psychopathology of emotional disorders, he has been a statistical investigator/consultant on numerous federally funded research grants. He was a member of the *DSM-5* Research Planning Committee and was an Advisor to the *DSM-5* Anxiety Disorders Workgroup. Currently, his research has focused on dimensional approaches to emotional disorder classification, the role of temperament in the psychopathology and longitudinal course of emotional disorders, and diathesis-stress models of emotional disorders (e.g., interaction of novel candidate genes and life stress on the temporal course of emotional disorders).

**David H. Barlow** received his PhD from the University of Vermont in 1969 and has published over 500 articles and chapters as well as over 60 books and clinical manuals, mostly in the area of emotional disorders and clinical research methodology. The book and manuals have been translated into over 20 languages, including Arabic, Chinese, Hindi, and Russian. He was formerly Professor of Psychiatry at the University of Mississippi Medical Center and Professor of Psychiatry and Psychology at Brown University and founded clinical psychology internships in both settings. He was also Distinguished Professor in the Department of Psychology at the University at Albany, State University of New York. Currently, he is Professor of Psychology and Psychiatry, and Founder and Director Emeritus, of the Center for Anxiety and Related Disorders at Boston University. Dr. Barlow is the recipient of the 2000 American Psychological Association (APA) Distinguished Scientific Award for the Applications of Psychology, and the James McKeen Cattell Fellow Award from the Association for Psychological Science, honoring individuals for their lifetime of significant intellectual achievements in applied psychological research. He is also the recipient of the 2008 Career/Lifetime Achievement Award, Association for Behavioral and Cognitive Therapies (ABCT); and recipient of the 2000 Distinguished Scientific Contribution Award from the Society of Clinical Psychology of the APA. He also received an award in appreciation of outstanding achievements from the General Hospital of the Chinese People's Liberation Army, Beijing, with an appointment as Honorary Visiting Professor of Clinical Psychology. During the 1997–1998 academic year, he was Fritz Redlich Fellow at the Center for Advanced Study in Behavioral Sciences, in Palo Alto, California. Other awards include Career Contribution Awards from the Massachusetts, California, and Connecticut Psychological Associations; the 2004 C. Charles Burlingame Award from the Institute of Living in Hartford, Connecticut; the First Graduate Alumni Scholar Award from the Graduate College, University of Vermont; the Masters and Johnson Award, from the Society for Sex Therapy and Research; a certificate of appreciation for contributions to women in clinical psychology from the Society of Clinical Psychology, Section IV: the Clinical Psychology of Women; and a MERIT award from the National Institute of Mental Health for long-term contributions to the clinical research effort. His research has been continually funded by the National Institutes of Health for over 40 years. In 2004 he received an Honorary Doctorate in Humane Letters from the Massachusetts School of Professional Psychology, and in 2006, the American Board of Professional Psychology's Distinguished Service Award to the Profession of Psychology. He is Past-President of the Society of Clinical Psychology of the APA and the ABCT, Past-Editor of several journals including *Clinical Psychology: Science and Practice* and *Behavior Therapy*, and currently Editor-in-Chief of the "Treatments that Work" series for Oxford University Press. He was a member of the *DSM-IV* Task Force of the American Psychiatric Association, and a Co-Chair of the Work Group for revising the anxiety disorder categories. He is a Diplomate in Clinical Psychology of the American Board of Professional Psychology and maintains a private practice.

Name: ______________________________

Address: ____________________________

______________________________

Phone (home): ________________________

(work): ________________________

(cell): ________________________

**Indicate preferred contact phone number with asterisk*

Email: ______________________________

Date of Birth: ________________________

Sex: ____ M ____ F

Date of Interview: ____________________

Interviewer: _________________________

Family Income: _______________________

Number of Dependents: ________________

Veteran Status: ______________________

Insurance Plan: ______________________

Fee for Interview: ____________________

Ethnicity (check one):

____ Hispanic or Latino

____ Non-Hispanic/Latino

Race (check all that apply):

____ American Indian/Alaska Native

____ Asian

____ Native Hawaiian/Other Pacific Islander

____ Black/African American

____ White/Caucasian

____ Other

Religion: ____________________________

Marital Status:

| | Date: |
|---|---|
| ____ Single | |
| ____ Married | ____________ |
| ____ Cohabiting | ____________ |
| ____ Separated | ____________ |
| ____ Divorced | ____________ |
| ____ Widowed | ____________ |
| ____ Other | ____________ |

Number of Prior Marriages: ______________

Dates: _______________________________

Children:

| Age | Sex | At Home? |
|---|---|---|
| ____ | ____ | Y N |
| ____ | ____ | Y N |
| ____ | ____ | Y N |
| ____ | ____ | Y N |

Occupational History:

Patient:

________________________ (present/date)

________________________ (prior/date)

________________________

Spouse/partner

________________________ (present/date)

________________________ (prior/date)

________________________

Highest Education:

Patient: ____________________________

Spouse/partner: ______________________

The interview should begin with a brief introduction and explanation of the purpose of the interview. A brief description of the presenting complaint should be obtained. In this section, a preliminary determination of the presence of panic attacks, phobic avoidance, depression, and chronic worry should be made (as well as any medical difficulties or life circumstances that may be associated with the presenting complaints).

**I will be asking you a number of questions about different areas of your life. First, I would like to get a general idea of what sorts of problems you have been having recently. What have they been?**

______________________________________________

______________________________________________

**If you had to identify one issue, what would you say is the <u>main</u> reason that brought you here today?** (record patient's response verbatim)

______________________________________________

______________________________________________

## STRESSORS

**In the past year, have you had any changes in or difficulties with** (distinguish episodic and ongoing stressors)**:**

**Family?** ______________________________________________

______________________________________________

______________________________________________

**Social Life/Romantic Relationships?** ______________________________________________

______________________________________________

______________________________________________

**Work/School?** ______________________________________________

______________________________________________

______________________________________________

**Financial?** ______________________________________________

______________________________________________

______________________________________________

**Health (self)?** ______________________________________________

______________________________________________

______________________________________________

**Health (significant others)?** ______________________________________________

______________________________________________

______________________________________________

**Loss of Loved One?** ______________________________________________

______________________________________________

______________________________________________

**Legal Matters/Police/Accidents?** ______________________________________________

______________________________________________

AFTER BRIEF INQUIRY:

**Before we discuss the problems that brought you here today in more detail, I'd like to get information on your medical background and on any previous treatments you have received for anxiety, depression, or other emotional difficulties.**

# MEDICAL/TREATMENT HISTORY

## I. HISTORY OF PSYCHOLOGICAL/PSYCHIATRIC TREATMENT

1a. **Have you ever been hospitalized for anxiety, depression, substance use, or another emotional problem?**

YES ____ NO ____

Date Hospital/Doctor Reason Treatment/Medication

_______________________________________________

_______________________________________________

_______________________________________________

b. **Have you ever received any outpatient therapy or evaluations for any emotional or personal difficulties?**

YES ____ NO ____

Date Clinic/Doctor Reason Treatment

_______________________________________________

_______________________________________________

_______________________________________________

_______________________________________________

2a. **Are you <u>currently</u> taking any medications for anxiety, depression, or another emotional problem?** (include sleep medications)

YES ____ NO ____

Date Clinic/Doctor Reason Medication/Dose

_______________________________________________

_______________________________________________

_______________________________________________

_______________________________________________

b. **Have you <u>ever</u> taken any medications for anxiety, depression, or another emotional problem?** (include sleep medications)

YES ____ NO ____

Date Clinic/Doctor Reason Medication/Dose

_______________________________________________

_______________________________________________

_______________________________________________

_______________________________________________

If CURRENT or PAST history of psychotropic medication use, ask:

c. **Have you ever experienced problems with these medications such as side effects, withdrawal problems, etc.?**

YES ____ NO ____

If YES, specify: ______________________________

## II. MEDICAL HISTORY

1a. **What is your height?** ____________ b. **What is your weight?** ____________

2a. **Do you have a physician/clinic that you see regularly to receive medical care, physical examinations, etc.?**

YES ____ NO ____

Name/address of physician or clinic:

______________________________

______________________________

b. **Are you currently being treated for any physical disease or condition?**

YES ____ NO ____

If YES, specify: ______________________________

3a. **When was your last physical exam?** ______________________________

b. **What were the results of this exam?** ______________________________

______________________________

4a. **Have you ever had surgery, or been advised to have surgery?**

YES ____ NO ____

| Date | Hospital/Doctor | Reason | Comments/Complications |
|---|---|---|---|
| | | | |
| | | | |
| | | | |

b. **Have you ever had to be hospitalized for a physical problem?**

YES ____ NO ____

| Date | Hospital/Doctor | Reason | Comments/Complications |
|---|---|---|---|
| | | | |
| | | | |
| | | | |

c. **Have you ever had a concussion or any head injury?**

YES ____ NO ____

| Date | Hospital/Doctor | Reason | Comments/Complications |
|---|---|---|---|
| | | | |
| | | | |
| | | | |

5. **Have you ever been diagnosed with any of the following?**

| | Yes | No | Date | Treatment/Comments |
|---|---|---|---|---|
| a. Diabetes | ___ | ___ | | |
| b. Heart problems | ___ | ___ | | |
| c. High/low blood pressure | ___ | ___ | | |
| d. Epilepsy | ___ | ___ | | |
| e. Cancer | ___ | ___ | | |
| f. Thyroid disease | ___ | ___ | | |
| g. Other hormonal problem | ___ | ___ | | |
| h. Asthma | ___ | ___ | | |
| i. Other respiratory problem | ___ | ___ | | |
| j. Migraines | ___ | ___ | | |
| k. Stroke | ___ | ___ | | |
| l. Neurological disorders | ___ | ___ | | |
| m. Ulcer/GI disorders | ___ | ___ | | |
| n. Blood disorders (e.g., hypoglycemia) | ___ | ___ | | |
| o. HIV/AIDS | ___ | ___ | | |
| p. **Any other disease?** | ___ | ___ | | |

q. **Is there a history in your biological family (e.g., father, mother, siblings) of any of these problems?**

YES ____ NO ____

If YES, specify: ______________________________

6. **Do you have any allergies (hay fever, penicillin, medications, etc.)?** YES ____ NO ____

If YES, specify: ______________________________

7. **Are you a smoker?** YES ____ NO ____

If YES, **Packs/day?**: _______________ **How many years?** _______________

## MEDICAL/TREATMENT HISTORY

8. **Have you had any of the following tests in the last five years?; Did these tests indicate any abnormalities?**

| | Yes | No | Date | Results |
|---|---|---|---|---|
| a. Electrocardiogram (EKG) | ___ | ___ | | ______________________ |
| b. EEG or brain scan | ___ | ___ | | ______________________ |
| c. CT scan or MRI | ___ | ___ | | ______________________ |
| d. Chest X-ray | ___ | ___ | | ______________________ |
| e. Blood test | ___ | ___ | | ______________________ |
| f. Urine test | ___ | ___ | | ______________________ |

9. FEMALES:

a. **Date last menstrual period began:** ______________________

b. **Any reason to believe you may be pregnant?** YES ____ NO ____

c. **History of any gynecological problems, miscarriages, etc.?** YES ____ NO ____

If YES to b. or c., specify: ______________________

**Now I am going to ask you more questions about some specific kinds of emotional problems that may or may not apply to you. We have already touched briefly on some of them, but now I would like to get more details.**

# PANIC DISORDER

## I. INITIAL INQUIRY

1a. **Do you currently have times when you feel a sudden rush of intense fear or discomfort?**

YES ____ NO ____

If YES, skip to 2a.

b. If NO, **Have you ever had times when you have felt a sudden rush of intense fear or discomfort?**

YES ____ NO ____

If YES, **When was the most recent time this occurred?**

______________________________________________________________

******************************************************************************************

If YES to either 1a. or 1b., or uncertain, continue inquiry.
Otherwise skip to **AGORAPHOBIA** (p. 16).

******************************************************************************************

2a. **In what kinds of situation(s) [do/did] you have these feelings?; Where [are/were] you most likely to have these feelings?**

Current: ______________________________________________________

______________________________________________________________

Past: ________________________________________________________

______________________________________________________________

b. **[Do/did] you ever have these feelings come from "out of the blue," for no apparent reason, or in situations where you did not expect them to occur?**

Current: YES ____ NO ____

Past: YES ____ NO ____

If patient indicates the presence of unexpected panic symptoms, further inquiry is necessary to determine if these symptoms occur in a number of situational contexts or whether the symptoms are limited to a particular type of situation (e.g., as can occur in Social Anxiety Disorder or Specific Phobia).

3. **How long [does/did] it usually take for the rush of fear or discomfort to reach its peak level?**

Current: _______ minutes

Past: _______ minutes

4. **How long [does/did] the fear or discomfort usually last at its peak level?**

Current: _______ minutes

Past: _______ minutes

******************************************************************************************

If no evidence of panic attacks,
Skip to **AGORAPHOBIA** (p. 16).

******************************************************************************************

5a. **When did these symptoms first begin?** ______________________________

b. **After these symptoms began, [have/did] you experience(d) them continuously, or [have there been/were there] periods of time after the symptoms began that you were not bothered by them?** [To foster subsequent inquiry, try to begin to establish dates of onset/remission and presence of more than one discrete episodes of disturbance.]

______________________________

______________________________

## II. SYMPTOM RATINGS

CURRENT panic attack ratings should be obtained for patients who report current panic attacks. If patient only reports past panic attacks, initially obtain PAST panic attack ratings. In these cases, CURRENT symptom ratings should be obtained after establishing a past diagnosis of Panic Disorder (or "with panic attacks" specifier for other disorders) in the PAST EPISODE section (e.g., to determine partial/full remission). If there is evidence of separate episodes, inquire about the presence of discrete episodes of disturbance (e.g., "**Since the panics began, have there been periods of time when you were not bothered by them?**"). For patients endorsing both current and past episodes, CURRENT symptom ratings should be obtained first and PAST ratings should be obtained after completing the CURRENT EPISODE section. If it is determined a symptom can be subsumed by another disorder, rate it "0."

For the diagnosis of Panic Disorder, rate symptoms only for panic attacks that occur unexpectedly, in a variety of situations, under the PD column. Use the Other columns (OTH1, OTH2) to rate panic attacks occurring in context of other disorders; e.g., for the "with panic attacks" specifier when assigning diagnoses such as Social Anxiety Disorder and Specific Phobia. When the Other columns are used, indicate the disorder that is being rated in the space provided.

Rate the severity of each symptom that is typical of the most recent period of attacks and, when appropriate, what characterized a typical attack in a separate past episode of disturbance. If a symptom is experienced during only some attacks (i.e., does not typically occur during an attack), enclose the rating in parentheses.

*DSM-5* defines a panic attack as a discrete period of intense fear or discomfort, in which at least 4 of the symptoms listed below develop abruptly and reach a peak within minutes. If typical attacks do not include 4 symptoms, determine if any attack has included 4 symptoms.

Use the following inquiry when rating symptoms:

CURRENT EPISODE:

**During this current period of attacks, do you usually experience ______ during the attacks?**
**How distressing/severe is the symptom to you?**

If there is any doubt about whether the symptom is typical, ask:

**Do you experience this nearly every time you have an attack?**

PAST EPISODE:

**During that period of time in ______** (dates), **did you usually experience ______ during the attacks?**
**How distressing/severe was the symptom to you?**

If there is any doubt about whether the symptom is typical, ask:

**Did you experience this nearly every time you had an attack?**

Rate the severity of typical symptoms using the following scale:

0------------1------------2------------3------------4------------5------------6------------7------------8

None Mild Moderate Severe Very severe

Other Disorder 1 (OTH1): ____________________ Other Disorder 2 (OTH2): ____________________

| | CURRENT PD | CURRENT OTH1 | CURRENT OTH2 | PAST PD | PAST OTH1 | PAST OTH2 | COMMENTS |
|---|---|---|---|---|---|---|---|
| 1. Palpitations, pounding heart, or accelerated heart rate | ___ | ___ | ___ | ___ | ___ | ___ | ____________ |
| 2. Sweating | ___ | ___ | ___ | ___ | ___ | ___ | ____________ |
| 3. Trembling or shaking | ___ | ___ | ___ | ___ | ___ | ___ | ____________ |
| 4. Shortness of breath or smothering sensations | ___ | ___ | ___ | ___ | ___ | ___ | ____________ |
| 5. Feelings of choking | ___ | ___ | ___ | ___ | ___ | ___ | ____________ |
| 6. Chest pain or discomfort | ___ | ___ | ___ | ___ | ___ | ___ | ____________ |
| 7. Nausea or stomach distress | ___ | ___ | ___ | ___ | ___ | ___ | ____________ |
| 8. Dizziness, unsteady feelings, lightheadedness, or faintness | ___ | ___ | ___ | ___ | ___ | ___ | ____________ |
| 9. Chills or heat sensations | ___ | ___ | ___ | ___ | ___ | ___ | ____________ |
| 10. Numbing or tingling sensations | ___ | ___ | ___ | ___ | ___ | ___ | ____________ |
| 11. Feelings of unreality or being detached from oneself | ___ | ___ | ___ | ___ | ___ | ___ | ____________ |
| 12. Fear of losing control | ___ | ___ | ___ | ___ | ___ | ___ | ____________ |
| 13. Fear of going crazy | ___ | ___ | ___ | ___ | ___ | ___ | ____________ |
| 14. Fear of dying | ___ | ___ | ___ | ___ | ___ | ___ | ____________ |

If the patient reports 4 or more symptoms per typical attack, ask:

**[Do/did] you ever have attacks when you [have/had] a sudden rush of fear or discomfort that [is/was] accompanied by only one or two of these symptoms?**

Current: YES ____ NO ____

Past: YES ____ NO ____

If YES, repeat inquiry and circle the severity ratings in the appropriate column to indicate symptoms present during a typical Limited Symptom Attack.

If the patient reports less than 4 symptoms per typical attack, ask:

**[Do/did] you ever have attacks when you [have/had] a sudden rush of fear or discomfort that [is/was] accompanied by four or more of these symptoms?**

Current: YES ____ NO ____

Past: YES ____ NO ____

If YES, circle the ratings for symptoms that characterize a Limited Symptom Attack and repeat inquiry to determine the potential presence (and severity) of additional symptoms that may characterize a Full Panic Attack.

## III. CURRENT EPISODE

**Now I want to ask you some questions about the panic attacks you are currently experiencing.**

1a. **How many panic attacks have you had in the past month?**

______ Full _____ Limited

b. **How many panic attacks have you had in the past 6 months?**

______ Full _____ Limited

2a. **In the last month, how much have you been worried or concerned about having another panic attack or about the potential consequences of having another attack** (circle rating)?

0------------1------------2------------3------------4------------5------------6------------7------------8

| No worry | Rarely worried | Occasionally worried | Frequently worried | Constantly worried |
|---|---|---|---|---|

If no evidence of persistent concern/worry about panic over past month, ask: **Since your first attack, has there ever been a period of a month or more when you were worried that you might have more attacks?**

YES ____ NO ____

If YES, when was this?

FROM _________ TO ________

b. **Specifically, what types of things do you anticipate happening as the result of the attacks?** (Inquire about immediate and long-term consequences.)

________________________________________________

________________________________________________

c. **Have the attacks caused you to change your behavior/lifestyle in any way?**

YES ____ NO ____

If YES, **How so?** ________________________________________________

________________________________________________

Inquire about the following areas of behavior/lifestyle change. After recording the nature of the maladaptive behavior change, rate severity using the scale below.

0------------1------------2------------3------------4------------5------------6------------7------------8

| None | Mild | Moderate | Severe | Very severe |
|---|---|---|---|---|

Situational avoidance: Rating: _____

________________________________________________

Interoceptive sensitivity/avoidance (e.g., physical exertion, sex, caffeine, expressing strong emotions, hot places, thrilling movies, activities that heighten awareness of bodily sensations): Rating: _____

________________________________________________

Safety signals (e.g., medications, people, access to telephones/car): Rating: _____

________________________________________________

Distraction (loud music, keeping TV on, staying involved in activities): Rating: _____

______________________________________________

Lifestyle changes (e.g., reduction in "stressful" activities or workload): Rating: _____

______________________________________________

3. **In what ways have the panics interfered with your life** (e.g., daily routine, job, social activities)?; **How much are you bothered about having the attacks?**

______________________________________________

______________________________________________

Rate interference: _______________ distress: _______________

0------------1------------2------------3------------4------------5------------6------------7------------8

None Mild Moderate Severe Very severe

4a. **Can you recall your first panic attack?**

YES ____ NO ____

If YES, **When did it happen?** _______________ Month _______________ Year

b. **Where were you when your first attack occurred?**

______________________________________________

c. **Were you under any type of stress during this time?**

YES ____ NO ____

**What was happening in your life at the time?**

______________________________________________

______________________________________________

d. **Were you taking any type of drug at the time of your first attack?** (include alcohol/caffeine)

YES ____ NO ____

If YES, specify type/amount: ______________________________________________

5. **When did the panic attacks become a problem?** (Determine when the panic attacks and accompanying symptoms met *DSM-5* threshold; i.e., when the attacks became recurrent and were accompanied by persistent concern about additional attacks and maladaptive behavior change.)

______________________________________________

Date of Disorder Onset: _______________ Month _______________ Year

6. **Have you been regularly taking any types of drugs during this current period of panic attacks?**

YES ____ NO ____

Specify (type; amount; dates of use): ______________________________________________

______________________________________________

7. **At the time of or since these panic attacks began, did you have any physical condition such as inner ear problems, heart problems, pregnancy, hyperthyroidism, or hypoglycemia?**

YES ____ NO ____

Specify (type; date of onset/remission): ____________________

____________________

8a. **Besides this current period of panic attacks, have there been other, separate periods of time before this when you had these attacks** (inquire about discrete, previous episodes of panic that were followed by periods of remission)?

YES ____ NO ____

b. If YES, **When did this/these past period(s) of attacks occur?**

____________________

If YES, go back to 2a. in INITIAL INQUIRY (p. 7).

If NO, skip to AGORAPHOBIA (p. 16).

## IV. PAST EPISODE(S)

**Now I want to ask you a series of questions about the past period of attacks that began roughly in ______________ and ended roughly in ______________** (specify dates).

List dates (onset/remission) corresponding to period(s) of inquiry:

Past Episode #1: FROM ______________ TO ______________

Past Episode #2: FROM ______________ TO ______________

1. **During that period of time in** ______________ (dates), **how many panic attacks did you typically have per month?**

Past Episode #1: ______________ Full ______________ Limited

Past Episode #2: ______________ Full ______________ Limited

2a. **During that period of time in** ______________ (dates), **how much were you worried or concerned about having another panic attack or about the potential consequences of having another attack?**

0------------1------------2------------3------------4------------5------------6------------7------------8

| No worry | Rarely worried | Occasionally worried | Frequently worried | Constantly worried |
|---|---|---|---|---|

Past Episode #1: __________

Past Episode #2: __________

If no evidence of persistent concern/worry over period ask, **Was there ever a period of a month a more during this time when you were worried that you might have more attacks?**

#1: YES ____ NO ____

#2: YES ____ NO ____

If YES, **When was this?**

#1: FROM ______________ TO ______________

#2: FROM ______________ TO ______________

b. **Specifically, what types of things did you anticipate happening as the result of the attacks?** (Inquire about immediate and long-term consequences.)

#1: ______________________________

#2: ______________________________

c. **Did the attacks cause you to change your behavior/lifestyle in any way?**

#1: YES ____ NO ____

#2: YES ____ NO ____

If YES, **How so?** #1 ______________________________

#2: ______________________________

Inquire about the following areas of behavior/lifestyle change. After recording the nature of the maladaptive behavior change, rate severity using the scale below.

0------------1------------2------------3------------4------------5------------6------------7------------8

None Mild Moderate Severe Very severe

Situational avoidance: Rating #1: _____ #2: _____

#1: ______________________________

#2: ______________________________

Interoceptive sensitivity/avoidance (e.g., physical exertion, sex, caffeine, expressing strong emotions, hot places, thrilling movies, activities that heighten awareness of bodily sensations):

Rating #1: _____ #2: _____

#1: ______________________________

#2: ______________________________

Safety signals (e.g., medications, people, access to telephones/car): Rating #1: _____ #2: _____

#1: ______________________________

#2: ______________________________

Distraction (loud music, keeping TV on, staying involved in activities): Rating #1: _____ #2: _____

#1: ______________________________

#2: ______________________________

Lifestyle changes (e.g., reduction in "stressful" activities or workload): Rating #1: _____ #2: _____

#1: ______________________________

#2: ______________________________

3. **In what ways did the panics interfere with your life** (e.g., daily routine, job, social activities)**?; How much were you bothered about having the attacks?**

#1: ______________________________

#2: ______________________________

#1: Rate interference: ______________ distress: ______________

#2: Rate interference: ______________ distress: ______________

0------------1------------2------------3------------4------------5------------6------------7------------8

None Mild Moderate Severe Very severe

4a. **Can you recall your first panic attack that began the period of attacks in** _______________ (year)?

#1: YES ____ NO ____

#2: YES ____ NO ____

If YES, **When did it happen?**

#1: _______________ Month _______________ Year

#2: _______________ Month _______________ Year

b. **Where were you when this attack occurred?**

#1: ________________________________________

#2: ________________________________________

c. **Were you under any type of stress during this time?**

#1: YES ____ NO ____

#2: YES ____ NO ____

**What was happening in your life at the time?**

#1: ________________________________________

#2: ________________________________________

d. **Were you taking any type of drug at the time of your first attack?** (include alcohol/caffeine)

#1: YES ____ NO ____

#2: YES ____ NO ____

If YES, specify type/amount: #1: ________________________________________

#2: ________________________________________

5. **During that period of time in** _______________ (dates), **when did the panic attacks become a problem?** (Determine when the panic attacks and accompanying symptoms met *DSM-5* threshold; i.e., when the attacks became recurrent and were accompanied by persistent concern about additional attacks and maladaptive behavior change.)

#1: Date of Disorder Onset: _______________ Month _______________ Year

#2: Date of Disorder Onset: _______________ Month _______________ Year

6. **During this period of time, were you regularly taking any types of drugs?**

#1: YES ____ NO ____

#2: YES ____ NO ____

Specify (type; amount; dates of use) #1: ________________________________________

#2: ________________________________________

7. **At the time of or since the panic attacks began during this period, did you have any physical condition such as inner ear problems, heart problems, pregnancy, hyperthyroidism, or hypoglycemia?**

#1: YES ____ NO ____

#2: YES ____ NO ____

Specify (type; date of onset/remission) #1: ____________________

#2: ____________________

8a. **When were the attacks no longer a problem, in that they stopped occurring and you were no longer worried or concerned about having more attacks?**

#1: ____________________

#2: ____________________

Date of remission: #1: ____________ Month ____________ Year

#2: ____________ Month ____________ Year

b. **Can you recall any reasons why the attacks stopped occurring or why you were no longer worried about them?**

#1: YES ____ NO ____

#2: YES ____ NO ____

#1: ____________________

#2: ____________________

9a. **Prior to or after this period of panic attacks, have there been other, separate periods of time that we haven't covered when you were having these attacks?**

YES ____ NO ____

b. If YES, **When did this/these other period(s) of attacks occur?**

____________________

If YES, ascertain whether a separate period of disturbance has existed of unexpected panic attacks (perhaps using items from INITIAL INQUIRY); if so, readminister items in PAST EPISODE for Past Episode #2.

If NO, skip to AGORAPHOBIA (p. 16).

## AGORAPHOBIA

### I. INITIAL INQUIRY

1a. **Do you currently feel panicky in any situations or avoid them because you might feel panicky?**

YES ____ NO ____

If YES, **What are some of the situations you fear or avoid?**

______________________________________________________________________

Skip to 1c.

b. If NO, **Have you <u>ever</u> felt panicky about entering situations or avoided them because of panic?**

YES ____ NO ____

If NO, continue to 1c.

If YES, **What were some of the situations you feared or avoided?**

______________________________________________________________________

Continue to 1c.

c. **Are you currently apprehensive about entering situations due to the fear you may develop unpleasant or embarrassing symptoms such as diarrhea, vomiting, dizziness, or incontinence?**

YES ____ NO ____

If NO, continue to 1d.

If YES, **What symptoms do you fear might arise in these situations?**

______________________________________________________________________

**What were some of the situations you feared or avoided due to these symptoms?**

______________________________________________________________________

Skip to 2a.

d. **Have you ever been apprehensive about entering situations due to the fear you may develop unpleasant or embarrassing symptoms such as diarrhea, vomiting, dizziness, or incontinence?**

YES ____ NO ____

If YES, **What symptoms did you fear might arise in these situations?**

______________________________________________________________________

**What were some of the situations you feared or avoided due to these symptoms?**

______________________________________________________________________

IF NO to 1a. through 1d., skip to SITUATION RATINGS.

IF YES to 1a., 1b., 1c., or 1d., ask:

2a. **When did these symptoms first begin?** ______________________________

b. **After these symptoms began, [have/did] you experience(d) them continuously, or [have there been/were there] periods of time after the symptoms began that you were not bothered by them?** [To foster subsequent inquiry, try to begin to establish dates of onset/remission and presence of more than one discrete episodes of disturbance.]

______________________________________________________________________

______________________________________________________________________

## II. SITUATION RATINGS

CURRENT agoraphobia situation ratings should be obtained for: (a) patients who do not report current or past agoraphobia; and (b) patients who report current agoraphobic fear/avoidance only. If patient only reports past agoraphobic fear/avoidance, obtain PAST agoraphobic situation ratings. In these cases, CURRENT symptom ratings should then be obtained after establishing either: (a) a past diagnosis of Agoraphobia in the PAST EPISODES section (e.g., to determine partial/full remission); or (b) the absence of past Agoraphobia diagnoses after administration of the PAST EPISODES section or determining the absence of clinically significant agoraphobia symptoms after administering PAST agoraphobia situation ratings. If there is evidence of separate episodes, inquire about the presence of discrete episodes of disturbance (e.g., "**Since the fear began, have there been periods of time when you were not bothered by it?**"). For patients endorsing both current and past episodes, CURRENT agoraphobia situation ratings should be obtained first and PAST ratings should be obtained after completing the CURRENT EPISODE section. Ratings should pertain only to the anticipation of panic or other unpleasant or embarrassing symptoms (e.g., diarrhea). Apprehension/avoidance due to other conditions (e.g., Specific Phobia, Social Anxiety Disorder) should be rated "0." Use space for comments to record other clinically useful information (e.g., frequency with which feared situation arises).

Use the following inquiry when rating the situations on Apprehension (APP) and Avoidance (AVD):

**How apprehensive [are/were] you to enter this situation?; How often [do/did] you avoid this situation?; [Does/did] having someone with you make a difference in terms of how comfortable you [feel/felt] in these situations?**

0------------1------------2------------3------------4------------5------------6------------7------------8

| 0 | 2 | 4 | 6 | 8 |
|---|---|---|---|---|
| No avoidance or escape/No apprehension | Occasional avoidance or escape/Mild apprehension | Moderate: may enter alone/ Moderate apprehension | Severe: will rarely enter alone; must be accompanied/ Severe apprehension | Very Severe: never enters even with safe person/ Very severe apprehension |

| | CURRENT | | PAST | | |
|---|---|---|---|---|---|
| | APP | AVD | APP | AVD | COMMENTS |
| Transportation | | | | | |
| 1. Driving locally | ___ | ___ | ___ | ___ | ________________ |
| 2. Driving long distances; on freeways/interstates | ___ | ___ | ___ | ___ | ________________ |
| 3. Passenger in a car | ___ | ___ | ___ | ___ | ________________ |
| 4. Public transportation (e.g., buses, trains, ships) | ___ | ___ | ___ | ___ | ________________ |
| 5. Air travel | ___ | ___ | ___ | ___ | ________________ |
| Open Spaces | | | | | |
| 6. Bridges | ___ | ___ | ___ | ___ | ________________ |
| 7. Parking lots; parks | ___ | ___ | ___ | ___ | ________________ |
| 8. Large arenas | ___ | ___ | ___ | ___ | ________________ |

| | CURRENT | | PAST | | |
|---|---|---|---|---|---|
| | APP | AVD | APP | AVD | COMMENTS |
| Enclosed Places | | | | | |
| 9. Grocery stores | ___ | ___ | ___ | ___ | ___ |
| 10. Malls | ___ | ___ | ___ | ___ | ___ |
| 11. Theaters/cinemas | ___ | ___ | ___ | ___ | ___ |
| 12. Restaurants | ___ | ___ | ___ | ___ | ___ |
| 13. Small shops | ___ | ___ | ___ | ___ | ___ |
| 14. Place of worship | ___ | ___ | ___ | ___ | ___ |
| 15. Doctor/dentist visits | ___ | ___ | ___ | ___ | ___ |
| 16. Hairdresser/barber | ___ | ___ | ___ | ___ | ___ |
| 17. Elevators | ___ | ___ | ___ | ___ | ___ |
| 18. Small rooms/tunnels | ___ | ___ | ___ | ___ | ___ |
| Lines/Crowds | | | | | |
| 19. Standing in line | ___ | ___ | ___ | ___ | ___ |
| 20. Being in crowds | ___ | ___ | ___ | ___ | ___ |
| Away from home (alone) | | | | | |
| 21. Going out of town | ___ | ___ | ___ | ___ | ___ |
| 22. Taking walks | ___ | ___ | ___ | ___ | ___ |
| 23. Leaving the house | ___ | ___ | ___ | ___ | ___ |
| Other Situations | | | | | |
| 24. Being at home alone | ___ | ___ | ___ | ___ | ___ |
| 25. Work/school | ___ | ___ | ___ | ___ | ___ |
| 26. Other ___ | ___ | ___ | ___ | ___ | ___ |
| 27. Other ___ | ___ | ___ | ___ | ___ | ___ |

*****************************************************************************************

If no evidence of fear or avoidance of any of these situations is obtained,
Skip to **SOCIAL ANXIETY DISORDER** (p. 22).

*****************************************************************************************

## III. CURRENT EPISODE

If evidence of a discrete past episode, preface inquiry in this section with: **Now I want to ask you a series of questions about this <u>current</u> period of apprehension/avoidance of situations that began roughly in** ___ (specify dates).

1. **Do you feel anxious nearly every time you enter these situations or when you are faced with the possibility of having to enter these situations?**

YES ___ NO ___

2. **Are there any sorts of things that you carry with you, or things that you do before going out that help you feel more comfortable?** [Inquire about safety signals such as medication bottles, cellphones, having access to own car, books/printed coping instructions, drinks, materials relating to getting sick in public (e.g., paper towels).]

______________________________________________

______________________________________________

3. **In what ways has the fear/avoidance of these situations interfered with your life** (e.g., daily routine, job, social activities)?**; How much are you bothered about being fearful or avoidant of these situations?**

______________________________________________

______________________________________________

Rate interference: ______________ distress: ______________

0------------1------------2------------3------------4------------5------------6------------7------------8

None | Mild | Moderate | Severe | Very severe

4. **When did your fear and avoidance of situations become a problem?** (Determine when the agoraphobic avoidance met *DSM-5* threshold; i.e., when the fear/avoidance of two or more types of situations became sufficiently prominent to cause clinically significant interference and distress.)

______________________________________________

Date of Disorder Onset: ______________ Month ______________ Year

5. **Have you been regularly taking any types of drugs during this current period of situational fear and avoidance?**

YES ____ NO ____

Specify (type; amount; dates of use): ______________________________

______________________________________________

6. **At the time of or since these symptoms began, did you have any physical condition such as inner ear problems, heart problems, inflammatory bowel disease, or Parkinson's disease?**

YES ____ NO ____

Specify (type; date of onset/remission): ______________________________

______________________________________________

7a. **Besides this current period of situational fear and avoidance, have there been other, separate periods of time before this when you had these symptoms** (inquire about discrete, previous episodes of agoraphobia that were followed by periods of remission)**?**

YES ____ NO ____

b. If YES, **When did this/these past period(s) of situational fear and avoidance occur?**

______________________________________________

If YES, go back to SITUATIONAL RATINGS, PAST (p. 17).

If NO, skip to SOCIAL ANXIETY DISORDER (p. 22).

## IV. PAST EPISODES

**Now I want to ask you a series of questions about the past period of apprehension/avoidance of situations that began roughly in ______________ and ended roughly in ______________** (specify dates):

List dates (onset/remission) corresponding to period(s) of inquiry:

Past Episode #1: FROM ______________ TO ______________

Past Episode #2: FROM ______________ TO ______________

1. **Did you feel anxious nearly every time you entered these situations or when you were faced with the possibility of having to enter these situations?**

   #1: YES ____ NO ____

   #2: YES ____ NO ____

2. **Were there any sorts of things that you carried with you, or things that you did before going out that helped you feel more comfortable?** [Inquire about safety signals such as medication bottles, cellphones, having access to own car, books/printed coping instructions, drinks, materials relating to getting sick in public (e.g., paper towels).]

   #1: ____________________________________________

   #2: ____________________________________________

3. **In what ways did the fear/avoidance of these situations interfere with your life** (e.g., daily routine, job, social activities)?; **How much were you bothered about being fearful or avoidant of these situations?**

   #1: ____________________________________________

   #2: ____________________________________________

   #1: Rate interference: ______________ distress: ______________

   #2: Rate interference: ______________ distress: ______________

   0------------1------------2------------3------------4------------5------------6------------7------------8

   None Mild Moderate Severe Very severe

4. **During that period of time in __________** (dates)**, when did your fear and avoidance of situations become a problem?** (Determine when the agoraphobic avoidance met *DSM-5* threshold; i.e., when the fear/avoidance of two or more types of situations became sufficiently prominent to cause clinically significant interference and distress.)

   #1: ____________________________________________

   #2: ____________________________________________

   #1: Date of Disorder Onset: ______________ Month ______________ Year

   #2: Date of Disorder Onset: ______________ Month ______________ Year

5. **Were you regularly taking any types of drugs during that period of situational fear and avoidance?**

   #1: YES ____ NO ____

   #2: YES ____ NO ____

   Specify (type; amount; dates of use) #1: ______________________________

   #2: ____________________________________________

6. **At the time of or since the symptoms began back in ________ (dates), did you have any physical condition such as inner ear problems, heart problems, inflammatory bowel disease, or Parkinson's disease?**

#1: YES ____ NO ____

#2: YES ____ NO ____

Specify (type; date of onset/remission) #1: ______________________________

#2: ______________________________

7a. **When was the fear/avoidance of situations no longer a problem, in that you felt comfortable entering all of these situations?**

#1: ______________________________

#2: ______________________________

Date of remission: #1: ____________ Month ____________ Year

#2: ____________ Month ____________ Year

b. **Can you recall any reasons why you began to feel comfortable entering these situations again?**

#1: YES ____ NO ____

#2: YES ____ NO ____

#1: ______________________________

#2: ______________________________

8a. **Prior to or after this past period, have there been other, separate periods of time that we haven't covered when you feared or avoided situations due to these feelings** (inquire about discrete, other episodes of Agoraphobia that were separated by periods of remission)**?**

YES ____ NO ____

b. If YES, **When did this/these other period(s) of situational fear and avoidance occur?**

______________________________

If YES, ascertain whether a separate period of disturbance has existed of agoraphobic fear/avoidance (using items from INITIAL INQUIRY, SITUATION RATINGS, p. 16–17); if so, readminister items for Past Episode #2.

If NO, go back to SITUATION RATINGS to obtain CURRENT ratings (p. 17); then skip to SOCIAL ANXIETY DISORDER (p. 22).

# SOCIAL ANXIETY DISORDER

## I. INITIAL INQUIRY

1a. **Currently, in social situations where you might be observed or evaluated by others or when you are meeting new people, do you feel fearful, anxious, or nervous?**

YES ____ NO ____

b. **Currently, are you overly concerned that you may do and/or say something that might embarrass or humiliate yourself in front of others, or that others may think badly of you?**

YES ____ NO ____

If NO to 1a. and 1b., continue to 1c.

If YES to either 1a. or 1b., skip to 2a.

c. **Have you ever been anxious in social situations or were you ever overly concerned about embarrassing or humiliating yourself in front of others?**

YES ____ NO ____

IF NO to 1a., 1b., and 1c., skip to SITUATION RATINGS.

IF YES to 1a., 1b., or 1c., ask:

2a. **When did these symptoms first begin?** ______________________________

b. **After these symptoms began, [have/did] you experience(d) them continuously, or [have there been/were there] periods of time after the symptoms began that you were not bothered by them?** [To foster subsequent inquiry, try to begin to establish dates of onset/remission and presence of more than one discrete episodes of disturbance.]

______________________________

______________________________

## II. SITUATION RATINGS

**I am going to describe some situations of this type and ask how you would feel in each situation and to what extent you avoid these situations.**

CURRENT social situation ratings should be obtained for: (a) patients who do not report current or past social anxiety; and (b) patients who report current social anxiety only. If patient only reports past social anxiety, initially obtain PAST social situation ratings. In these cases, CURRENT symptom ratings should then be obtained after establishing either: (a) a past diagnosis of Social Anxiety Disorder in the PAST EPISODE section (e.g., to determine partial/full remission); or (b) the absence of past Social Anxiety Disorder diagnoses after administration of the PAST EPISODE section or determining the absence of clinically significant social anxiety symptoms after administering PAST social situation ratings. If there is evidence of separate episodes, inquire about the presence of discrete episodes of disturbance (e.g., "**Since the fear began, have there been periods of time when you were not bothered by it?**"). For patients endorsing both current and past episodes, CURRENT social situation ratings should be obtained first and PAST ratings should be obtained after completing the CURRENT EPISODE section. Use Comments section to record other clinically useful information (e.g., frequency with which feared situation arises).

For each situation, make separate ratings for level of fear and degree of avoidance using the following scale:

| 0 | 1 | 2 | 3 | 4 | 5 | 6 | 7 | 8 |
|---|---|---|---|---|---|---|---|---|
| No fear/ Never avoids | | Mild fear/ Rarely avoids | | Moderate fear/ Sometimes avoids | | Severe fear/ Often avoids | | Very severe fear/ Always avoids |

CURRENT: **Currently, are you anxious in or do you avoid:**
PAST: **Have you ever been anxious in or do you avoid:**

| | CURRENT | | PAST | | |
|---|---|---|---|---|---|
| | FEAR | AVOID | FEAR | AVOID | COMMENTS |
| Performance | | | | | |
| 1. Giving a speech or presentation | ___ | ___ | ___ | ___ | ___ |
| 2. Introducing yourself to a group | ___ | ___ | ___ | ___ | ___ |
| 3. Performing in front of others (e.g., music, theater, sports) | ___ | ___ | ___ | ___ | ___ |
| 4. Writing in public (signing checks, filling out forms) | ___ | ___ | ___ | ___ | ___ |
| 5. Eating in public | ___ | ___ | ___ | ___ | ___ |
| 6. Using public restrooms | ___ | ___ | ___ | ___ | ___ |
| Social Interaction | | | | | |
| 7. Attending parties | ___ | ___ | ___ | ___ | ___ |
| 8. Participating at meetings/ classes | ___ | ___ | ___ | ___ | ___ |
| 9. Speaking with unfamiliar people | ___ | ___ | ___ | ___ | ___ |
| 10. Talking on the phone | ___ | ___ | ___ | ___ | ___ |
| 11. Dating situations | ___ | ___ | ___ | ___ | ___ |
| 12. Talking to persons in authority | ___ | ___ | ___ | ___ | ___ |
| 13. Being assertive: Refusing requests | ___ | ___ | ___ | ___ | ___ |
| Asking others to change their behavior | ___ | ___ | ___ | ___ | ___ |
| 14. Initiating a conversation | ___ | ___ | ___ | ___ | ___ |
| 15. Maintaining a conversation | ___ | ___ | ___ | ___ | ___ |
| Other | | | | | |
| 16. ___ | ___ | ___ | ___ | ___ | ___ |
| 17. ___ | ___ | ___ | ___ | ___ | ___ |

*************************************************************************************

If no evidence of fear/avoidance is obtained,
Skip to **SEPARATION ANXIETY DISORDER** (p. 28).

*************************************************************************************

## III. CURRENT EPISODE

If evidence of a discrete past episode, preface inquiry in this section with: **Now I want to ask you a series of questions about your current anxiety in social situations that began roughly in** _______________ (specify dates).

Complete for current episode of social anxiety that is potentially of clinical severity:

A. List most problematic situations: ____________________________________________

1. **What are you concerned will happen in these situations?** ____________________________________________

____________________________________________

2. **Do you feel anxious nearly every time you enter these situations or when you are faced with the possibility of having to enter these situations?**

YES ____ NO ____

3a. **Are you anxious about these situations because you are afraid that you will have a panic attack?**

YES ____ NO ____

If YES,

b. **Other than times when you are exposed to** _______________ (specify social situations), **have you experienced an unexpected rush of fear/anxiety?**

YES ____ NO ____

If YES, **Where has this occurred?** ____________________________________________

If YES to 3a. or 3b., consider whether fear could be subsumed under Panic Disorder/Agoraphobia. Also consider whether the "with panic attacks" specifier should be assigned with a diagnosis of Social Anxiety Disorder (i.e., administer panic attack symptom ratings in Panic Disorder section for Other Disorder, p. 9)

4a. **Has your current job or educational attainment been influenced by these fears?**

YES ____ NO ____

____________________________________________

____________________________________________

b. **In what other ways have these fears interfered with your life** (e.g., daily routine, job, social activities)?; **How much are you bothered by these fears?**

____________________________________________

____________________________________________

Rate interference: _______________ distress: _______________

0------------1------------2------------3------------4------------5------------6------------7------------8

None — Mild — Moderate — Severe — Very severe

5a. **When did your fear and avoidance of social situations become a problem?** (Determine when the social anxiety met *DSM-5* threshold; i.e., when the fear/avoidance of social situations became sufficiently prominent to cause clinically significant interference and distress.)

____________________________________________

Date of Disorder Onset: _______________ Month _______________ Year

b. **Can you recall anything that might have contributed to you feeling anxious about social situations?**

YES ____ NO ____

______________________________________________________________________

______________________________________________________________________

6. **Have you been regularly taking any types of drugs or medications during this current period of social fears and avoidance?**

YES ____ NO ____

Specify (type; amount; dates of use): ______________________________________________

______________________________________________________________________

7. **At the time of or since these symptoms began, did you have any physical condition such as stuttering, a neurological disorder, or a disorder that resulted in a change in your physical appearance or functioning?**

YES ____ NO ____

Specify (type; date of onset/remission): ______________________________________________

______________________________________________________________________

8a. **Besides this current period of social fears and avoidance, have there been other, separate periods of time before this when you had these symptoms** (inquire about discrete, previous episodes of Social Anxiety Disorder that were followed by periods of remission)**?**

YES ____ NO ____

b. If YES, **When did this/these past period(s) of social fears and avoidance occur?**

______________________________________________________________________

If YES, go back to SITUATION RATINGS, PAST (p. 23).

If NO, skip to SEPARATION ANXIETY DISORDER (p. 28)

## IV. PAST EPISODE

**Now I want to ask you a series of questions about anxiety in social situations that began roughly in _______________ and ended roughly in _______________** (specify dates).

Complete for past episode of social anxiety that was potentially of clinical severity:

A. List most problematic situations: ______________________________________________

1. **What were you concerned would happen in these situations?** ______________________________

______________________________________________________________________

2. **Did you feel anxious nearly every time you entered these situations or when you were faced with the possibility of having to enter these situations?**

YES ____ NO ____

3a. **Were you anxious about these situations because you were afraid you would have a panic attack?**

YES ____ NO ____

If YES,

b. **Other than times when you were exposed to** ______________ (specify social situations), **did you experience an unexpected rush of fear/anxiety?**

YES ____ NO ____

If YES, **Where did this occur?** ________________________________

If YES to 3a. or 3b., consider whether fear could be subsumed under Panic Disorder/Agoraphobia. Also consider whether the "with panic attacks" specifier should be assigned with a diagnosis of Social Anxiety Disorder (i.e., administer panic attack symptom ratings in Panic Disorder section for Other Disorder, p. 9)

4a. **Was your job or educational attainment influenced by these fears?**

YES ____ NO ____

________________________________

________________________________

b. **In what other ways did these fears interfere with your life** (e.g., daily routine, job, social activities)**?; How much were you bothered by these fears?**

________________________________

________________________________

Rate interference: ______________ distress: ______________

0------------1------------2------------3------------4------------5------------6------------7------------8

None Mild Moderate Severe Very severe

5a. **When did your fear and avoidance of social situations become a problem?** (Determine when the social anxiety met *DSM-5* threshold; i.e., when the fear/avoidance of social situations became sufficiently prominent to cause clinically significant interference and distress.)

________________________________

Date of Disorder Onset: ______________ Month ______________ Year

b. **Can you recall anything that might have contributed to you feeling anxious about social situations?**

YES ____ NO ____

________________________________

________________________________

6. **Were you regularly taking any types of drugs during this period of social fears and avoidance?**

YES ____ NO ____

Specify (type; amount; dates of use): ________________________________

________________________________

7. **At the time of or since these symptoms began, did you have any physical condition such as stuttering, a neurological disorder, or a disorder that resulted in a change in your physical appearance or functioning?**

YES ____ NO ____

Specify (type; date of onset/remission): ______________________________

______________________________

8a. **When was the fear/avoidance of social situations no longer a problem, in that you felt comfortable entering all of these situations?**

______________________________

Date of remission: ______________ Month ______________ Year

b. **Can you recall any reasons why you were no longer anxious about these situations?**

YES ____ NO ____

______________________________

______________________________

9a. **Prior to or after this period of anxiety in social situations, have there been other, separate periods of time that we haven't covered when you have had the same problems** (inquire about discrete, other episodes of Social Anxiety Disorder that were separated by periods of remission)**?**

YES ____ NO ____

b. If YES, **When did this/these other period(s) of social fears and avoidance occur?**

______________________________

If YES, go back to SITUATION RATINGS, PAST (p. 23).

If NO, go back to SITUATION RATINGS to obtain CURRENT ratings (p. 23); then skip to SEPARATION ANXIETY DISORDER (p. 28).

# SEPARATION ANXIETY DISORDER

## I. INITIAL INQUIRY

1a. **Currently, do you feel anxious or upset when you are faced with the prospect of being separated from home and/or from the people you are closest to** (e.g., parents, caretakers, family members)?

YES ____ NO ____

If NO, skip to 1c.

If YES, specify major attachment figure(s): ______________________________

If history of panic attacks or agoraphobia, ask:

b. **Is this anxiety about being away from home and/or loved ones due primarily to the concern that you might have a panic attack or experience other unpleasant physical symptoms?**

YES ____ NO ____

If NO, skip to 2a.

c. **Was there ever a time when you felt anxious or upset when you were faced with the prospect of being separated from home and/or from the people you were closest to** (e.g., parents, caretakers, family members)?

YES ____ NO ____

If YES, specify major attachment figure(s): ______________________________

If history of panic attacks or agoraphobia, ask:

d. **Was this anxiety about being away from home and/or loved ones due primarily to the concern that you might have a panic attack or experience other unpleasant physical symptoms?**

YES ____ NO ____

***************************************************************************************************

If evidence of separation anxiety is obtained, or uncertain, continue inquiry;
Otherwise, skip to **GENERALIZED ANXIETY DISORDER** (p. 33).

***************************************************************************************************

2a. **When did these symptoms first begin?** ______________________________

b. **After these symptoms began, [have/did] you experience(d) them continuously, or [have there been/were there] periods of time after the symptoms began that you were not bothered by them?** [To foster subsequent inquiry, try to begin to establish dates of onset/remission and presence of more than one discrete episodes of disturbance.]

______________________________

______________________________

## II. SYMPTOM RATINGS

CURRENT symptom ratings should be obtained for patients who report current separation anxiety only. If patient only reports past separation anxiety, initially obtain PAST symptom ratings. In these cases, CURRENT symptom ratings should be obtained after establishing a past diagnosis of Separation Anxiety Disorder in the PAST EPISODE section (e.g., to determine partial/full remission). If there is evidence of separate episodes, inquire about the presence of discrete episodes of disturbance (e.g., "**Since these concerns began, have there been periods of time when you were not bothered by them?**"). For patients endorsing both current and past episodes, CURRENT symptom ratings should be obtained first and PAST ratings should be obtained after completing the CURRENT EPISODE section. If it is determined a symptom can be subsumed by another disorder, rate it "0."

Rate the persistence/severity of each symptom using the scale below. If the symptom is present, provide further information as necessary.

| 0 | 1 | 2 | 3 | 4 | 5 | 6 | 7 | 8 |
|---|---|---|---|---|---|---|---|---|
| Never/ None | | Rarely/Mild | | Occasionally/ Moderate | | Frequently/ Severe | | Constantly/ Very Severe |

CURRENT: **During the past several months, has your anxiety about being away from __________** (specify home/major attachment figures) **been associated with the following:**

PAST: **During that time in _____** (specify dates), **was your anxiety about being away from __________** (specify home/major attachment figures) **associated with the following:**

| | CURRENT | PAST |
|---|---|---|
| 1. Distress when anticipating or experiencing being away from home or major attachment figures<br>______________________________ | ____ | ____ |
| 2. Worry about losing major attachment figures or about possible harm to them (e.g., illness, injury, disasters, death)<br>______________________________ | ____ | ____ |
| 3. Worry that a negative event will lead to sudden separation from a major attachment figure (e.g., getting lost, kidnapping, accident, illness)<br>______________________________ | ____ | ____ |
| 4. Reluctance or refusal to leave home to go to school, work, or elsewhere<br>______________________________ | ____ | ____ |
| 5. Fear or reluctance about being alone or without major attachment figures at home or in other settings<br>______________________________ | ____ | ____ |
| 6. Reluctance or refusal to sleep away from home, or to sleep without being near a major attachment figure<br>______________________________ | ____ | ____ |
| 7. Nightmares involving separation<br>______________________________ | ____ | ____ |
| 8. Physical symptoms (e.g., headache, stomach ache, nausea/vomiting) when separation from major attachment figures occurs or is anticipated<br>______________________________ | ____ | ____ |

*****************************************************************************************

If no evidence of clinically significant separation anxiety symptoms,
Skip to **GENERALIZED ANXIETY DISORDER** (p. 33).

*****************************************************************************************

## III. CURRENT EPISODE

1. **What are the main things you fear might happen if you are away from home or you are separated from your loved ones?**

______________________________________________________________________

______________________________________________________________________

2. **In what ways has your concerns about being away from home/loved ones interfered with your life** (e.g., daily routine, job, social activities)**?; How much are you bothered by these concerns?**

______________________________________________________________________

______________________________________________________________________

Rate interference: ______________ distress: ______________

0------------1------------2------------3------------4------------5------------6------------7------------8

None Mild Moderate Severe Very severe

3a. **When did your concerns about being away from home/loved ones become a problem?** (Determine when the separation anxiety disorder met *DSM-5* threshold; i.e., when the separation anxiety symptoms were sufficient in number and associated impairment/distress.)

______________________________________________________________________

Date of Disorder Onset: ______________ Month ______________ Year

b. **Can you recall anything that might have led to this problem?**

YES ____ NO ____

______________________________________________________________________

______________________________________________________________________

c. **Were you under any type of stress during this time?**

YES ____ NO ____

**What was happening in your life at the time?**

______________________________________________________________________

______________________________________________________________________

4a. **Besides this current period, have there been other, separate periods of time before this when you had persistent concerns about being away from home/loved ones** (inquire about discrete, previous episodes of separation anxiety disorder that were followed by periods of remission)**?**

YES ____ NO ____

b. If YES, **When did this/these past period(s) of separation concerns occur?**

______________________________________________________________________

If YES, go back to SYMPTOM RATINGS, PAST (p. 29).

If NO, skip to GENERALIZED ANXIETY DISORDER (p. 33).

## IV. PAST EPISODE

**Now I want to ask you a series of questions about the past period of concerns about being separated from home or loved ones that began roughly in _______________ and ended roughly in _______________** (specify dates).

1. **What were the main things you feared might happen if you were away from home or you were separated from your loved ones?**

   ______________________________________________________________________

   ______________________________________________________________________

2. **In what ways did your concerns about being away from home/loved ones interfere with your life** (e.g., school, social activities)**?; How much were you bothered by these concerns?**

   ______________________________________________________________________

   ______________________________________________________________________

   Rate interference: _______________ distress: _______________

   0------------1------------2------------3------------4------------5------------6------------7------------8

   None Mild Moderate Severe Very severe

3a. **When did your concerns about being away from home/loved ones become a problem?** (Determine when the Separation Anxiety Disorder met *DSM-5* threshold; i.e., when the separation anxiety symptoms were sufficient in number and associated impairment/distress.)

   ______________________________________________________________________

   Date of Disorder Onset: _______________ Month _______________ Year

b. **Can you recall anything that might have led to this problem?**

   YES ____ NO ____

   ______________________________________________________________________

   ______________________________________________________________________

c. **Were you under any type of stress during this time?**

   YES ____ NO ____

   **What was happening in your life at the time?**

   ______________________________________________________________________

   ______________________________________________________________________

4a. **When were the concerns about being away from home/loved ones no longer a problem, in that you were able to leave home and/or be apart from your loved ones without feeling anxious, worried, or upset?**

   Date of remission: _______________ Month _______________ Year

b. **Can you recall any reasons why this was no longer a problem for you?**

   YES ____ NO ____

   ______________________________________________________________________

   ______________________________________________________________________

5a. **Prior to or after this past period of concerns about being away from home/loved ones, have there been other, separate periods of time that we haven't covered when you had these same problems** (inquire about discrete, other episodes of Separation Anxiety Disorder that were separated by periods of remission)**?**

YES ____ NO ____

b. If YES, **When did this/these other period(s) of separation concerns occur?**

______________________________________________

If YES, go back to INITIAL INQUIRY/SYMPTOM RATINGS (p. 28).

If NO, skip to GENERALIZED ANXIETY DISORDER (p. 33).

# GENERALIZED ANXIETY DISORDER

## I. INITIAL INQUIRY

1a. **Over the last several months, have you been continually worried or anxious about a number of events or activities in your daily life?**

YES ____ NO ____

If NO, skip to 1b.

**What kinds of things do you worry about?** ______________________________

______________________________

Skip to 2a.

b. **Have you <u>ever</u> experienced an extended period when you were continually worried or anxious about a number of events or activities in your daily life?**

YES ____ NO ____

If NO, skip to WORRY RATINGS.

**What kinds of things do you worry about?** ______________________________

______________________________

IF NO to 1a. and 1b., skip to WORRY RATINGS.

IF YES to 1a. or 1b., ask:

2a. **When did these symptoms first begin?** ______________________________

b. **After these symptoms began, [have/did] you experience(d) them continuously, or [have there been/were there] periods of time after the symptoms began that you were not bothered by them?** [To foster subsequent inquiry, try to begin to establish dates of onset/remission and presence of more than one discrete episodes of disturbance.]

______________________________

______________________________

## II. WORRY RATINGS

### A. WORRY AREAS

**Now I want to ask you a series of questions about worry about several areas of life:**

CURRENT worry ratings should be obtained for: (a) patients who do not report worry; and (b) patients who report current worry only. If patient only reports past worry, initially obtain PAST worry ratings. In these cases, CURRENT symptom ratings should then be obtained after establishing either: (a) a past diagnosis of Generalized Anxiety Disorder in the PAST EPISODE section (e.g., to determine partial/full remission); or (b) the absence of past Generalized Anxiety Disorder diagnoses after administration of the PAST EPISODE section or determining the absence of clinically significant worry symptoms after administering PAST worry ratings. If there is evidence of <u>separate</u> episodes, inquire about the presence of <u>discrete</u> episodes of disturbance (e.g., "**Since the worry began, have there been periods of time when you were not bothered by it?**"). For patients endorsing both current and past episodes, CURRENT worry ratings should be obtained first and PAST ratings should be obtained after completing the CURRENT EPISODE section. Use the space below each worry area to record the specific content of the patient's worry (including information obtained previously from items 1a. and 1b.). Further inquiry will often be necessary to determine whether areas of worry are unrelated to a co-occurring disorder. If it is determined an area of worry can be subsumed totally by another disorder, rate this area as "0." Use Comments section to record clinically useful information (e.g., data pertaining to the discreteness of episodes, co-existing disorder with which the area of worry is related).

For each area of worry, make separate ratings of Excessiveness (i.e., frequency and intensity) and Uncontrollability using the scales and suggested queries below. In addition, for each area, inquire if the patient was bothered by the worry more days than not for at least 6 months using the query below.

EXCESSIVENESS:

0------------1------------2------------3------------4------------5------------6------------7------------8

| 0 | 2 | 4 | 6 | 8 |
|---|---|---|---|---|
| No worry/ No tension | Rarely worried/ Mild tension | Occasionally worried/Moderate tension | Frequently worried/Severe tension | Constantly worried/Extreme tension |

UNCONTROLLABILITY:

0------------1------------2------------3------------4------------5------------6------------7------------8

| 0 | 2 | 4 | 6 | 8 |
|---|---|---|---|---|
| Never/ No difficulty | Rarely/Slight difficulty | Occasionally/ Moderate difficulty | Frequently/ Marked difficulty | Constantly/ Extreme difficulty |

EXCESSIVENESS (EXC):

**How often [do/did] you worry about _______________?; If things [are/were] going well, [do/did] you still worry about _______________?; How much tension and anxiety [does/did] the worry about _______________ produce?**

UNCONTROLLABILITY (UNC):

**[Do/did] you find it hard to control the worry about _______________ in that it [is/was] difficult to stop worrying about it?; Is/was the worry about _______________ hard to control in that it [will/would] come into your mind when you [are/were] trying to focus on something else?**

MORE DAYS THAN NOT (DAY):

CURRENT: **During the past 6 months, have you been bothered by this worry more days than not?**
PAST: **Were you bothered by this worry more days than not for at least 6 months?**

| | CURRENT | | | PAST | | | |
|---|---|---|---|---|---|---|---|
| | EXC | UNC | DAY | EXC | UNC | DAY | COMMENTS |
| 1. Minor matters (e.g., day-to-day activities, errands) ___ ___ | ___ | ___ | Y N | ___ | ___ | Y N | ___ |
| 2. Work/school ___ ___ | ___ | ___ | Y N | ___ | ___ | Y N | ___ |
| 3. Health (self) ___ ___ | ___ | ___ | Y N | ___ | ___ | Y N | ___ |
| 4. Health (significant others, pets) ___ ___ | ___ | ___ | Y N | ___ | ___ | Y N | ___ |
| 5. Family ___ ___ | ___ | ___ | Y N | ___ | ___ | Y N | ___ |

| | CURRENT | | | PAST | | | |
|---|---|---|---|---|---|---|---|
| | EXC | UNC | DAY | EXC | UNC | DAY | COMMENTS |
| 6. Interpersonal relationships | ___ | ___ | Y N | ___ | ___ | Y N | ___ |
| 7. Finances | ___ | ___ | Y N | ___ | ___ | Y N | ___ |
| 8. Community/world affairs | ___ | ___ | Y N | ___ | ___ | Y N | ___ |
| 9. Other | ___ | ___ | Y N | ___ | ___ | Y N | ___ |
| 10. Other | ___ | ___ | Y N | ___ | ___ | Y N | ___ |

**B. WORRY BEHAVIORS** (OPTIONAL SECTION):

Rate the frequency/severity of maladaptive behaviors associated with worry using the inquiry and rating scale below.

0------------1------------2------------3------------4------------5------------6------------7------------8

Never    Rarely/Mild    Sometimes/Moderate    Often/Severe    Always/Very Severe

**To what extent do/did your worries affect your activities in the following ways:**

| | CURRENT | PAST |
|---|---|---|
| 1. Avoid activities/events with possible negative outcomes (e.g., authority figures, financial statements) | ___ | ___ |
| 2. Spend more time and effort preparing for activities/events with possible negative outcomes (e.g., presentations) | ___ | ___ |
| 3. Putting off actions or decisions (procrastination) | ___ | ___ |
| 4. Seeking reassurance from others | ___ | ___ |

********************************************************************************************

If no evidence of excessive/uncontrollable worry is obtained,
Skip to **OBSESSIVE-COMPULSIVE DISORDER** (p. 40).

********************************************************************************************

## III. CURRENT EPISODE

If evidence of a discrete past episode, preface inquiry in this section with: **Now I want to ask you a series of questions about your current period of worry that began roughly in** ______________ (specify dates).

List principal topics of worry: ____________________________________________

____________________________________________________________

1. **During the past 6 months, have you been bothered by these worries more days than not?**

   YES ____ NO ____

2. **On an average day over the past month, what percentage of the day did you feel worried?**

   _______ %

3. **Specifically, what types of things do you worry might happen regarding** ______________ (inquire for each principal area of worry)?

   ____________________________________________________________

   ____________________________________________________________

   ____________________________________________________________

4. **During the past 6 months, have you often experienced** ______________ **when you worried?; Has** ______________ **been present more days than not over the past 6 months?** (Do not record symptoms that are associated with other conditions such as panic, social anxiety, etc.)

   0-----------1-----------2-----------3-----------4-----------5-----------6-----------7-----------8

   None Mild Moderate Severe Very severe

| | SEVERITY | MORE DAYS THAN NOT |
|---|---|---|
| a. restlessness; feeling keyed up or on edge | _______ | Y N |
| b. being easily fatigued | _______ | Y N |
| c. difficulty concentrating or mind going blank | _______ | Y N |
| d. irritability | _______ | Y N |
| e. muscle tension | _______ | Y N |
| f. difficulty falling/staying asleep; restless/ unsatisfying sleep | _______ | Y N |

5. **In what ways have these worries and associated symptoms of tension/anxiety interfered with your life** (e.g., daily routine, job, social activities)?; **How much are you bothered by these worries?**

   ____________________________________________________________

   ____________________________________________________________

   Rate interference: ______________ distress: ______________

   0-----------1-----------2-----------3-----------4-----------5-----------6-----------7-----------8

   None Mild Moderate Severe Very severe

6a. **When did your worries become a problem?** (Determine when the generalized anxiety met *DSM-5* threshold; i.e., when the excessive/uncontrollable worries and associated symptoms became sufficiently prominent to cause clinically significant interference and distress.)

________________________________________________

Date of Disorder Onset: ______________ Month ______________ Year

b. **Can you recall anything that might have led to this problem?**

YES ____ NO ____

________________________________________________

________________________________________________

c. **Were you under any type of stress during this time?**

YES ____ NO ____

**What was happening in your life at the time?**

________________________________________________

________________________________________________

7. **Have you been regularly taking any types of drugs or medications during this current period when you've been having ongoing worries and feelings of tension/anxiety?**

YES ____ NO ____

Specify (type; amount; dates of use): ________________________________

________________________________________________

8. **At the time of or since these symptoms began, did you have any physical condition such as thyroid problems?**

YES ____ NO ____

Specify (type; date of onset/remission): ________________________________

________________________________________________

9a. **Besides this current period of worry and tension/anxiety, have there been other, separate periods of time before this when you had these symptoms** (inquire about discrete, previous episodes of Generalized Anxiety Disorder that were followed by periods of remission)?

YES ____ NO ____

b. If YES, **When did this/these past period(s) of worry and tension/anxiety occur?**

________________________________________________

If YES, go back to WORRY RATINGS, PAST (p. 34).

If NO, skip to OBSESSIVE-COMPULSIVE DISORDER (p. 40).

## IV. PAST EPISODE

**Now I want to ask you a series of questions about the past period of worry about these areas that began roughly in ______________ and ended roughly in ______________** (specify dates).

List principal topics of worry: ________________________________

________________________________________________

1. **During that time, were you bothered by these worries more days than not for at least 6 months?**

YES ____ NO ____

2. **On an average day during this period, what percentage of the day did you feel worried?**

_______ %

3. **Specifically, what types of things did you worry might happen regarding** ______________ (inquire for each principal area of worry)?

______________________________________________

______________________________________________

______________________________________________

4. **During that time, did you often experience ______________ when you worried?; Did you experience ______________ more days than not for at least 6 months during that time?** (Do not record symptoms that are associated with other conditions such as panic, social anxiety, etc.)

0------------1------------2------------3------------4------------5------------6------------7------------8

None Mild Moderate Severe Very severe

| | SEVERITY | MORE DAYS THAN NOT |
|---|---|---|
| a. restlessness; feeling keyed up or on edge | _______ | Y N |
| b. being easily fatigued | _______ | Y N |
| c. difficulty concentrating or mind going blank | _______ | Y N |
| d. irritability | _______ | Y N |
| e. muscle tension | _______ | Y N |
| f. difficulty falling/staying asleep; restless/ unsatisfying sleep | _______ | Y N |

5. **In what ways did these worries and associated symptoms of tension/anxiety interfere with your life** (e.g., daily routine, job, social activities)?; **How much were you bothered by these worries?**

______________________________________________

______________________________________________

Rate interference: ______________ distress: ______________

0------------1------------2------------3------------4------------5------------6------------7------------8

None Mild Moderate Severe Very severe

6a. **During that time, when did your worries become a problem?** (Determine when the generalized anxiety met *DSM-5* threshold; i.e., when the excessive/uncontrollable worries and associated symptoms became sufficiently prominent to cause clinically significant interference and distress.)

______________________________________________

Date of Disorder Onset: ______________ Month ______________ Year

b. **Can you recall anything that might have led to this problem?**

YES ____ NO ____

______________________________________________

______________________________________________

c. **Were you under any type of stress at this time?**

YES ____ NO ____

**What was happening in your life at the time?**

______________________________________________

______________________________________________

7. **During that past time period when you had ongoing worries and feelings of tension/anxiety, were you regularly taking any types of drugs or medications?**

YES ____ NO ____

Specify (type; amount; dates of use): ______________________________________________

______________________________________________

8. **At the time of or since the symptoms began, did you have any physical condition such as thyroid problems?**

YES ____ NO ____

Specify (type; date of onset/remission): ______________________________________________

______________________________________________

9a. **When were these symptoms no longer a problem, in that the worries and symptoms of tension/anxiety did not occur persistently, you weren't bothered by the worry or symptoms or found them hard to control, and they did not interfere with your life?**

______________________________________________

Date of remission: ______________ Month ______________ Year

b. **Can you recall any reasons why these worries and symptoms of tension/anxiety were no longer a problem for you?**

YES ____ NO ____

______________________________________________

______________________________________________

10a. **Prior to or after this period of worry and tension/anxiety, have there been other, separate periods of time that we haven't covered when you have had the same problems?** (inquire about discrete, other episodes of Generalized Anxiety Disorder that were followed by periods of remission)**?**

YES ____ NO ____

b. If YES, **When did this/these other period(s) of worry and tension/anxiety occur?**

______________________________________________

If YES, go back to WORRY RATINGS, PAST (p. 34).

If NO, go back to WORRY RATINGS to obtain CURRENT ratings (p. 34); then skip to OBSESSIVE-COMPULSIVE DISORDER (p. 40).

# OBSESSIVE-COMPULSIVE DISORDER

## I. INITIAL INQUIRY

1a. **Currently, are you bothered by thoughts, images, or impulses that keep recurring to you that seem inappropriate or nonsensical but that you can't stop from coming into your mind?**

YES ____ NO ____

If YES, specify: ______________________________

______________________________

b. **Currently, do you feel driven to repeat some behavior or to repeat something in your mind over and over again to try to feel less uncomfortable?**

YES ____ NO ____

If YES, specify: ______________________________

______________________________

If NO to 1a. and 1b., continue to 1c. and 1d.

If YES to either 1a. or 1b., skip to 2a.

c. **Have you ever had a time when you were bothered by thoughts, images, or impulses that kept recurring to you that seemed inappropriate or nonsensical?**

YES ____ NO ____

If YES, specify: ______________________________

______________________________

d. **Have you ever felt driven to repeat some behavior or to repeat something in your mind over and over again to try to feel less uncomfortable?**

YES ____ NO ____

If YES, specify: ______________________________

______________________________

IF NO to 1a. through 1d., skip to OBSESSIONS AND COMPULSIONS RATINGS.

IF YES to 1a., 1b., 1c., or or 1d., ask:

2a. **When did these symptoms first begin?** ______________________________

b. **After these symptoms began, [have/did] you experience(d) them continuously, or [have there been/were there] periods of time after the symptoms began that you were not bothered by them?** [To foster subsequent inquiry, try to begin to establish dates of onset/remission and presence of more than one discrete episodes of disturbance.]

______________________________

______________________________

## II. OBSESSIONS AND COMPULSIONS RATINGS

CURRENT ratings should be obtained for: (a) patients who do not report current or past obsessions or compulsions; and (b) patients who report current obsessions or compulsions only. If patient only reports past obsessions or compulsions, initially obtain PAST ratings. In these cases, CURRENT symptom ratings should then be obtained after establishing either: (a) a past diagnosis of Obsessive-Compulsive Disorder in the PAST EPISODE section (e.g., to determine partial/ full remission); or (b) the absence of past Obsessive-Compulsive Disorder diagnoses after administration of the PAST EPISODE section or determining the absence of clinically significant obsessions and compulsions after administering PAST ratings. If there is evidence of separate episodes, inquire about the presence of discrete episodes of disturbance (e.g., "**Since the symptom began, have there been periods of time when you were not bothered by it?**"). For patients endorsing both current and past episodes, CURRENT ratings should be obtained first and PAST ratings should be obtained after completing the CURRENT EPISODE section. Use the space below each item to record the specific content and nature of the patient's obsessions and/or compulsions (including information obtained previously from Items 1a. through 1d.). If it is determined that a symptom can be better accounted for by another disorder, rate it "0." Use Comments section to record clinically useful information (e.g., data pertaining to the discreteness of episodes, co-existing disorder with which a symptom is related).

A. OBSESSIONS:

For each obsession, make separate ratings of Persistence/Distress and Resistance using the scales and suggested queries below.

PERSISTENCE/DISTRESS (P/D):

**How often [does/did] _____________ enter your mind?; How distressing [is/was] it to you when _____________ [enters/entered] your mind?**

0------------1------------2------------3------------4------------5------------6------------7------------8

| 0 | 2 | 4 | 6 | 8 |
|---|---|---|---|---|
| Never/ No distress | Rarely/Mild distress | Occasionally/ Moderate distress | Frequently/ Marked distress | Constantly/ Extreme distress |

RESISTANCE (RES):

**How often [do/did] you attempt to get rid of _____________ by ignoring, suppressing, or trying to neutralize it/ them with some thought or action?**

0------------1------------2------------3------------4------------5------------6------------7------------8

| 0 | 2 | 4 | 6 | 8 |
|---|---|---|---|---|
| Never | Rarely | Occasionally | Frequently | Constantly |

| | CURRENT | | PAST | | |
|---|---|---|---|---|---|
| | P/D | RES | P/D | RES | COMMENTS |
| 1. Doubting (e.g., locks, turning off appliances, completion/accuracyof tasks) ________________ | ___ | ___ | ___ | ___ | ________________ |
| 2. Contamination (e.g., contracting germs from doorknobs, toilets, money, etc.) ________________ | ___ | ___ | ___ | ___ | ________________ |
| 3. Nonsensical urges (e.g., shouting or undressing in public) ________________ | ___ | ___ | ___ | ___ | ________________ |

| | CURRENT | | PAST | | |
|---|---|---|---|---|---|
| | P/D | RES | P/D | RES | COMMENTS |
| 4. Aggressive urges (e.g., hurting oneself or others, destroying objects) ______ | ___ | ___ | ___ | ___ | ______ |
| 5. Unwanted sexual thoughts/images (e.g., distressing obscene thoughts or images) ______ | ___ | ___ | ___ | ___ | ______ |
| 6. Unwanted religious/Satanic thoughts/images (e.g., blasphemous thoughts/impulses) ______ | ___ | ___ | ___ | ___ | ______ |
| 7. Accidental harm to others (e.g., hurting someone unknowingly by poisoning, hitting with car, etc.) ______ | ___ | ___ | ___ | ___ | ______ |
| 8. Horrific images (e.g., mutilated bodies) ______ | ___ | ___ | ___ | ___ | ______ |
| 9. Nonsensical thoughts/images (e.g., numbers, letters, songs) ______ | ___ | ___ | ___ | ___ | ______ |
| 10. Other ______ | ___ | ___ | ___ | ___ | ______ |
| 11. Other ______ | ___ | ___ | ___ | ___ | ______ |

B. COMPULSIONS:

For each compulsion, make ratings of Frequency using the scale and suggested queries below.

FREQUENCY (FREQ):

**How often [are/were] you driven to perform such actions as ______________?**

0------------1------------2------------3------------4------------5------------6------------7------------8

Never — Rarely — Occasionally — Frequently — Constantly

| | CURRENT | | PAST | | |
|---|---|---|---|---|---|
| | FREQ | | FREQ | | COMMENTS |
| 1. Checking (e.g., locks, appliances, driving routes, important papers, waste baskets) ______ | ___ | ___ | ___ | ___ | ______ |
| 2. Washing (e.g., self, household objects) ______ | ___ | ___ | ___ | ___ | ______ |
| 3. Counting (e.g., certain letters or numbers, objects in the environment) ______ | ___ | ___ | ___ | ___ | ______ |

| | CURRENT FREQ | PAST FREQ | COMMENTS |
|---|---|---|---|
| 4. Internal repetition (e.g., phrases, words, prayers) ____________ | ___ ___ | ___ ___ | ____________ |
| 5. Adhering to rules or behavioral sequences (e.g., ordering/symmetry, ritualistic acts, adhering to specific daily routine) ____________ | ___ ___ | ___ ___ | ____________ |
| 6. Other ____________ | ___ ___ | ___ ___ | ____________ |
| 7. Other ____________ | ___ ___ | ___ ___ | ____________ |

************************************************************************************************

If no evidence of obsessions or compulsions is obtained,
Skip to **BODY DYSMORPHIC DISORDER** (p. 49).

************************************************************************************************

## III. CURRENT EPISODE

A. OBSESSIONS

If no evidence of obsessions has been obtained, skip to Compulsions (p. 44)

If evidence of a discrete past episode, preface inquiry in this section with: **Now I want to ask you a series of questions about this current period of repetitive thoughts, images, or impulses that began roughly in ______________** (specify dates).

List principal obsessions: 1: ____________________________________________

2: ____________________________________________

Inquire for each obsession:

1a. **On the average day over the past month, what percentage of the day were the thoughts/impulses/images about ______________ in your mind?**

#1: ________ % #2: ________ % Overall: ________ %

b. If uncertain: **Are these thoughts/impulses/images typically in your mind for at least an hour a day?**

YES ____ NO ____

2a. **While the thought/impulse/image about ______________ is in your mind, how strongly do you believe that it is true** (0–100 scale where 0 = not at all and 100 = completely)?

#1: ________ % #2: ________ %

b. **For this current period of time when you've been bothered by these thoughts/images/impulses about ______________, how strongly did you believe that they were true, even during times when they were not in your mind** (0–100 scale)?

#1: ________ % #2: ________ %

3. **How do these thoughts/images/impulses about ______________ come into your mind** (ascertain whether patient recognizes that obsessions are a product of his/her own mind)**?**

________________________________________________________________________

If evidence of thought insertion, **Are these thoughts/images/impulses ever imposed by something outside of you?**

YES ____ NO ____

If YES, specify ____________________________________________________________

B. COMPULSIONS

If no evidence of compulsions has been obtained, skip to "C. Current Episode (Obsessions and/or Compulsions)"; p. 45.

If evidence of a discrete past episode, preface inquiry in this section with: **Now I want to ask you a series of questions about this current period of repetitive behaviors or mental actions that began roughly in ______________** (specify dates).

List principal compulsions: 1: __________________________________________________

2: __________________________________________________

Inquire for each compulsion:

1a. **On the average day over the past month, what percentage of the day were you ______________?**

#1: _______ % #2: _______ % Overall: _______ %

b. If uncertain: **Do you typically spend at least an hour a day performing these behaviors/mental actions?**

YES ____ NO ____

2. **Do you feel that repeating these behaviors/mental actions doesn't make sense or takes up more time than is really necessary?**

YES ____ NO ____

Specify: ____________________________________________________________

If NO, **At any time during this current period when you've been bothered by these behaviors/ mental acts, did you feel that they didn't make sense or took up more time than necessary?**

YES ____ NO ____

Specify: ____________________________________________________________

3a. **How often do you resist carrying out these behaviors/mental acts?**

________________________________________________________________________

b. **How anxious do you feel if you can't or don't carry out these acts?**

________________________________________________________________________

c. **What do you worry might happen if you don't carry out these acts?**

________________________________________________________________________

C. CURRENT EPISODE (OBSESSIONS AND/OR COMPULSIONS)

1. **In what ways have these repetitive thoughts/images/impulses/behaviors interfered with your life** (e.g., daily routine, job, social activities)**?; How much are you bothered by these symptoms?**

______________________________________________

______________________________________________

Rate interference: ____________ distress: ____________

0------------1------------2------------3------------4------------5------------6------------7------------8

None Mild Moderate Severe Very severe

2a. **When did your repetitive thoughts/images/impulses/behaviors become a problem?** (Determine when the obsessive-compulsive symptoms met *DSM-5* threshold; i.e., when the obsessions and compulsions became time-consuming and/or sufficiently prominent to cause clinically significant interference and distress.)

______________________________________________

Date of Disorder Onset: ____________ Month ____________ Year

b. **Can you recall anything that might have led to this problem?**

YES ____ NO ____

______________________________________________

______________________________________________

c. **Were you under any type of stress during this time?**

YES ____ NO ____

**What was happening in your life at the time?**

______________________________________________

______________________________________________

3. **Have you been regularly taking any types of drugs or medications during this current period when you've been having repetitive thoughts/images/impulses/behaviors?**

YES ____ NO ____

Specify (type; amount; dates of use): ______________________________

______________________________________________

4. **At the time of or since these symptoms began, did you have any physical condition?**

YES ____ NO ____

Specify (type; date of onset/remission): ______________________________

______________________________________________

5a. **Besides this current period of repetitive thoughts/images/impulses/behaviors, have there been other, separate periods of time before this when you had these symptoms** (inquire about discrete, previous episodes of Obsessive-Compulsive Disorder that were followed by periods of remission)**?**

YES ____ NO ____

b. If YES, **When did this/these past period(s) of repetitive thoughts/images/impulses/behaviors occur?**

______________________________________________

If YES, go back to OBSESSIONS AND COMPULSIONS RATINGS, PAST (p. 41).

If NO, skip to BODY DYSMORPHIC DISORDER (p. 49).

## IV. PAST EPISODE

A. OBSESSIONS

If no evidence of obsessions has been obtained, skip to Compulsions (p. 46)

**Now I want to ask you a series of questions about the past period of repetitive thoughts, images, or impulses that began roughly in ______________ and ended roughly in ______________** (specify dates).

List principal obsessions: 1: ______________________________

2: ______________________________

Inquire for each obsession:

1a. **On the average day during this period, what percentage of the day were the thoughts/ impulses/images about ______________ in your mind?**

#1: ________ % #2: ________ % Overall: ________ %

b. If uncertain: **Were these thoughts/impulses/images typically in your mind for at least an hour a day?**

YES ____ NO ____

2a. **While the thought/impulse/image about ______________ was in your mind, how strongly did you believe that it was true** (0–100 scale where 0 = not at all and 100 = completely)?

#1: ________ % #2: ________ %

b. **During that period of time when you were bothered by these thoughts/images/impulses about ______________, how strongly did you believe that they were true, even during times when they were not in your mind** (0–100 scale)?

#1: ________ % #2: ________ %

3. **How did these thoughts/images/impulses about ______________ come into your mind?** (Ascertain whether patient recognizes that obsessions were a product of his/her own mind.)

______________________________________________

If evidence of thought insertion, **Were these thoughts/images/impulses ever imposed by something outside of you?**

YES ____ NO ____

If YES, specify ______________________________

B. COMPULSIONS

If no evidence of compulsions has been obtained, skip to "C. Past Episode (Obsessions and/or Compulsions)"; p. 47.

**Now I want to ask you a series of questions about the past period or repetitive behaviors or mental actions that began roughly in ______________ and ended roughly in ______________** (specify month/year).

List principal compulsions: 1: ____________________

2: ____________________

Inquire for each compulsion:

1a. **On the average day during that period, what percentage of the day were you ______________?**

#1: ________ % #2: ________ % Overall: ________ %

b. If uncertain: **Did you typically spend at least an hour a day performing these behaviors/mental actions?**

YES ____ NO ____

2. **Did you feel that repeating these behaviors/mental actions didn't make sense or took up more time than was really necessary?**

YES ____ NO ____

Specify: ____________________

If NO, **At any time during this past period when you've been bothered by these behaviors/mental acts, did you feel that they didn't make sense or took up more time than necessary?**

YES ____ NO ____

Specify: ____________________

3a. **How often did you resist carrying out these behaviors/mental acts?**

____________________

b. **How anxious did you feel if you couldn't or didn't carry out these acts?**

____________________

c. **What did you worry might happen if you didn't carry out these acts?**

____________________

C. PAST EPISODE (OBSESSIONS AND/OR COMPULSIONS)

1. **In what ways did these repetitive thoughts/images/impulses/behaviors interfere with your life** (e.g., daily routine, job, social activities)**?; How much were you bothered about having these symptoms?**

____________________

____________________

Rate interference: ______________ distress: ______________

0-----------1-----------2-----------3-----------4-----------5-----------6-----------7-----------8

None Mild Moderate Severe Very severe

2a. **During that time, when did your repetitive thoughts/images/impulses/behaviors become a problem?** (Determine when the obsessive-compulsive symptoms met *DSM-5* threshold; i.e., when the obsessions and compulsions became time-consuming and/or sufficiently prominent to cause clinically significant interference and distress.)

____________________

Date of Disorder Onset: ______________ Month ______________ Year

b. **Can you recall anything that might have led to this problem?**

YES ____ NO ____

______________________________________________________________________

______________________________________________________________________

c. **Were you under any type of stress during this time?**

YES ____ NO ____

**What was happening in your life at the time?**

______________________________________________________________________

______________________________________________________________________

3. **During that past period of time when you were having these repetitive thoughts/images/impulses/ behaviors, were you regularly taking any types of drugs** (include drugs of abuse, medication)**?**

YES ____ NO ____

Specify (type; amount; dates of use): ______________________________________

______________________________________________________________________

4. **At the time of or since the symptoms began, did you have any physical condition?**

YES ____ NO ____

Specify (type; date of onset/remission): ____________________________________

______________________________________________________________________

5a. **When were these symptoms no longer a problem, in that they no longer were time-consuming or occurred repeatedly, you were not bothered by the symptoms, and they did not interfere with your life?**

______________________________________________________________________

Date of remission: ______________ Month ______________ Year

b. **Can you recall any reasons why these symptoms subsided?**

YES ____ NO ____

______________________________________________________________________

______________________________________________________________________

6a. **Prior to or after this period of repetitive thoughts/images/impulses/behaviors, have there been other, separate periods of time that we haven't covered when you have had the same problems** (inquire about discrete, other episodes of Obsessive-Compulsive Disorder that were separated by periods of remission)**?**

YES ____ NO ____

b. If YES, **When did this/these other period(s) of repetitive thoughts/images/impulses/behaviors occur?**

______________________________________________________________________

If YES, go back to OBSESSIONS AND COMPULSIONS RATINGS, PAST (p. 41).

If NO, go back to OBSESSIONS AND COMPULSIONS RATINGS to obtain CURRENT ratings (p. 41); then skip to BODY DYSMORPHIC DISORDER (p. 49).

## BODY DYSMORPHIC DISORDER

### I. INITIAL INQUIRY

1a. **Currently, have you been overly concerned or preoccupied about some aspect of your physical appearance** (e.g., skin, hair, nose, body build or symmetry)**?**

YES ____ NO ____

If NO, skip to 1b.

**What aspects of your physical appearance have you been concerned about?**

______________________________________________

______________________________________________

Skip to 2a.

b. **Have you ever been persistently concerned or preoccupied about some aspect of your physical appearance?**

YES ____ NO ____

If YES, **What aspects of your physical appearance were you concerned about?**

______________________________________________

______________________________________________

*****************************************************************************************************

If YES to either 1a. or 1b., or uncertain, continue inquiry.
Otherwise, skip to **SPECIFIC PHOBIA** (p. 53).

*****************************************************************************************************

2a. **When did these concerns first begin?** ______________________________

b. **After these concerns began, [have/did] you experience(d) them continuously, or [have there been/were there] periods of time after the concerns began that you were not bothered by them?** [To foster subsequent inquiry, try to begin to establish dates of onset/remission and presence of more than one discrete episodes of disturbance.]

______________________________________________

______________________________________________

### II. CURRENT EPISODE

If evidence of a discrete past episode, preface inquiry in this section with: **Now I want to ask you a series of questions about this current period of time when you have been preoccupied with ______________** (specify body concern)**, that began roughly in ______________** (specify dates).

List body areas of concern: ______________________________________________

1. **On an average day, what percentage of the day are you focused on your concerns about ________?**

_______ %

2a. **Are there any actions you perform regularly in response to your concerns about ________** (e.g., mirror checking, excessive grooming, hiding area, skin picking, reassurance seeking)?

YES ____ NO ____

Specify: ____________________________________________

____________________________________________

____________________________________________

IF YES,

b. **On an average day, what percentage of the day do you spend engaging in these behaviors/actions?**

_______ %

3. **In what ways have these concerns about ________ interfered with your life** (e.g., daily routine, job, social activities)?; **How much are you bothered by these concerns?**

____________________________________________

____________________________________________

Rate interference: ______________ distress: ______________

0------------1------------2------------3------------4------------5------------6------------7------------8

None Mild Moderate Severe Very severe

4a. **Currently, how strongly do you think your beliefs about ________ are true** (0–100 scale where 0 = not at all and 100 = completely)?

_______ %

b. **Is there any evidence you can think of that your beliefs about ________ are not true?**

YES ____ NO ____

If YES, have patient specify: ____________________________________________

____________________________________________

c. **Have other people noticed, or remarked to you about, this aspect of your appearance?**

YES ____ NO ____

Specify: ____________________________________________

____________________________________________

5a. **When did your concerns about ________ become a problem?** (Determine when the body dysmorphic symptoms met *DSM-5* threshold; i.e., when the preoccupation about physical appearance became sufficiently prominent to cause clinically significant interference and distress.)

____________________________________________

Date of Disorder Onset: ______________ Month ______________ Year

b. **Can you recall anything that might have led to this problem?**

YES ____ NO ____

____________________________________________

____________________________________________

6a. **Besides this current period of concerns about __________, have there been other, separate periods of time before this when you had persistent concerns about this or another aspect of your physical appearance** (inquire about discrete, previous episodes of Body Dysmorphic Disorder that were followed by periods of remission)**?**

YES ____ NO ____

b. If YES, **When did this/these past period(s) of appearance-related concerns occur?**

____________________________________________________________

If YES, go back to INITIAL INQUIRY/PAST EPISODE (pp. 49, 51).

If NO, skip to SPECIFIC PHOBIA (p. 53)

## III. PAST EPISODE

**Now I want to ask you a series of questions about the past period of time when you were preoccupied with** _______________ (specify body concern)**, that began roughly in** _______________ (specify dates).

List body areas of concern: ____________________________________________________

1. **During that time, on average, what percentage of the day were you focused on your concerns about ________?**

_______ %

2a. **Were there any actions you performed regularly in response to your concerns about __________** (e.g., mirror checking, excessive grooming, hiding area, skin picking, reassurance seeking)**?**

YES ____ NO ____

Specify: ________________________________________________________

____________________________________________________________

____________________________________________________________

IF YES,

b. **On an average day, what percentage of the day did you spend engaging in these behaviors/actions?**

_______ %

3. **In what ways did these concerns about __________ interfere with your life** (e.g., daily routine, job, social activities)**?; How much were you bothered by these concerns?**

____________________________________________________________

____________________________________________________________

Rate interference: _______________ distress: _______________

0------------1------------2------------3------------4------------5------------6------------7------------8

None | Mild | Moderate | Severe | Very severe

4a. **At the time, how strongly did you think your beliefs about __________ were true** (0–100 scale where 0 = not at all and 100 = completely)**?**

________ %

b. **Was there any evidence you could think of at the time that your beliefs about _________ were not true?**

YES ____ NO ____

If YES, have patient specify: ______________________________________________

______________________________________________

c. **At the time, did other people notice, or remark to you about, this aspect of your appearance?**

YES ____ NO ____

Specify: ______________________________________________

______________________________________________

5a. **When did your concerns about _________ become a problem?** (Determine when the body dysmorphic symptoms met *DSM-5* threshold; i.e., when the preoccupation about physical appearance became sufficiently prominent to cause clinically significant interference and distress.)

______________________________________________

Date of Disorder Onset: ______________ Month ______________ Year

b. **Can you recall anything that might have led to this problem?**

YES ____ NO ____

______________________________________________

______________________________________________

6a. **When did this stop being a problem for you, in that you were no longer preoccupied with your concerns about _________, and these concerns did not cause you to feel distressed or prompt you to engage in repeated appearance-related behaviors/actions?**

Date of remission: ______________ Month ______________ Year

b. **Can you recall any reasons why these concerns were no longer a problem for you?**

YES ____ NO ____

______________________________________________

______________________________________________

7a. **Prior to or after this period of concerns about _________, have there been other, separate periods of time we haven't covered when you had persistent concerns about this or another aspect of your physical appearance** (inquire about discrete, other episodes of Body Dysmorphic Disorder that were separated by periods of remission)?

YES ____ NO ____

b. If YES, **When did this/these other period(s) of appearance-related concerns occur?**

______________________________________________

If YES, go back to INITIAL INQUIRY (p. 49).

If NO, skip to SPECIFIC PHOBIA (p. 53).

# SPECIFIC PHOBIA

## I. INITIAL INQUIRY

For each situation, make separate ratings for level of fear and degree of avoidance using the following scale:

| 0 | 2 | 4 | 6 | 8 |
|---|---|---|---|---|
| No fear/ Never avoids | Mild fear/ Rarely avoids | Moderate fear/ Sometimes avoids | Severe fear/ Often avoids | Very severe fear/ Always avoids |

For each situation, inquire for both current and past episodes:

**Currently, do you fear or do you avoid such things as:**
**Have you ever feared or avoided such things as:**

If patient endorses a current specific fear, when inquiring about past fears of the same object/situation, this inquiry should be for the presence of discrete episodes of disturbance (e.g., "**Since the fear began, have there been periods of time when you were not bothered by it?**"). Use space for comments to record other clinically useful information (e.g., frequency with which feared situation arises).

| | CURRENT | | PAST | | |
|---|---|---|---|---|---|
| | FEAR | AVOID | FEAR | AVOID | COMMENTS |
| Animals | | | | | |
| 1. Dogs | ___ | ___ | ___ | ___ | ___ |
| 2. Snakes | ___ | ___ | ___ | ___ | ___ |
| 3. Spiders | ___ | ___ | ___ | ___ | ___ |
| 4. Bees/insects | ___ | ___ | ___ | ___ | ___ |
| 5. Other ___ | ___ | ___ | ___ | ___ | ___ |
| Natural Environment | | | | | |
| 6. Heights | ___ | ___ | ___ | ___ | ___ |
| 7. Storms | ___ | ___ | ___ | ___ | ___ |
| 8. Water | ___ | ___ | ___ | ___ | ___ |
| Blood-Injury-Injection (self or others) | | | | | |
| 9. Blood from minor cut | ___ | ___ | ___ | ___ | ___ |
| 10. Receiving injections | ___ | ___ | ___ | ___ | ___ |
| 11. Having blood drawn | ___ | ___ | ___ | ___ | ___ |
| 12. Invasive dental/medical procedures | ___ | ___ | ___ | ___ | ___ |
| Situational | | | | | |
| 13. Air travel | ___ | ___ | ___ | ___ | ___ |
| 14. Elevators/enclosed places | ___ | ___ | ___ | ___ | ___ |
| 15. Driving | ___ | ___ | ___ | ___ | ___ |
| Other | | | | | |
| 16. Choking | ___ | ___ | ___ | ___ | ___ |
| 17. Vomiting | ___ | ___ | ___ | ___ | ___ |

| | CURRENT | | PAST | | |
|---|---|---|---|---|---|
| | FEAR | AVOID | FEAR | AVOID | COMMENTS |
| 18. Contracting an illness | ___ | ___ | ___ | ___ | ____________________ |
| 19. Childhood fears (e.g., loud sounds, costumed characters) | ___ | ___ | ___ | ___ | ____________________ |
| 20. Other ____________________ | ___ | ___ | ___ | ___ | ____________________ |

************************************************************************************************

If no evidence is found for fear/avoidance,
Skip to **POSTTRAUMATIC STRESS DISORDER** (p. 60).

************************************************************************************************

## II. CURRENT EPISODES

Complete for each specific fear that is potentially of clinical severity:

If evidence of a discrete past episode, preface inquiry in this section with: **Now I want to ask you a series of questions about your current specific fears.**

A. Specific Fear #1: ____________________________________________

1. **What are you concerned will happen in this situation?** ____________________________________________

____________________________________________

2. **Do you feel anxious nearly every time you enter this situation or when you are faced with the possibility of having to enter this situation?**

YES ____ NO ____

3. **Does the anxiety occur as soon as you enter the situation or are about to enter the situation, or is the anxiety sometimes delayed or unexpected?**

IMMEDIATE ____ DELAYED ____

4a. **Are you anxious about these situations because you are afraid that you will have a panic attack?**

YES ____ NO ____

If YES,

b. **Other than times when you are exposed to** ______________ (specify phobic situation), **have you experienced an unexpected rush of fear/anxiety?**

YES ____ NO ____

If YES, **Where has this occurred?** ____________________________________________

If YES to 4a. or 4b., consider whether fear could be subsumed under Panic Disorder/Agoraphobia. Also consider whether the "with panic attacks" specifier should be assigned with a diagnosis of Specific Phobia (i.e., administer panic attack symptom ratings in Panic Disorder section for Other Disorder, p. 9).

5. **In what ways has this fear interfered with your life** (e.g., daily routine, job, social activities)**?; How much are you bothered by this fear?**

______________________________________________

______________________________________________

Rate interference: ______________ distress: ______________

0------------1------------2------------3------------4------------5------------6------------7------------8

None Mild Moderate Severe Very severe

6a. **When did your fear and avoidance of ________ become a problem?** (Determine when the Specific Phobia met *DSM-5* threshold; i.e., when the fear/avoidance of the object/situation became sufficiently prominent to cause clinically significant interference and distress.)

______________________________________________

Date of Disorder Onset: ______________ Month ______________ Year

b. **Can you recall anything that might have led to this fear?**

YES ____ NO ____

______________________________________________

______________________________________________

7a. **Besides this current period, have there been other, separate periods of time before this when you were bothered by this same fear** (inquire about discrete, previous episodes of Specific Phobia for this object/situation that were followed by periods of remission)**?**

YES ____ NO ____

b. If YES, **When did this/these past period(s) of fears and avoidance occur?**

______________________________________________

IF YES, go to INITIAL INQUIRY (PAST ratings, p. 53) and PAST EPISODES (p. 56)

B. Specific Fear #2: ______________________________________________

1. **What are you concerned will happen in this situation?** ______________________________

______________________________________________

2. **Do you feel anxious nearly every time you enter this situation or when you are faced with the possibility of having to enter this situation?**

YES ____ NO ____

3. **Does the anxiety occur as soon as you enter the situation or are about to enter the situation, or is the anxiety sometimes delayed or unexpected?**

IMMEDIATE ____ DELAYED ____

4a. **Are you anxious about these situations because you are afraid that you will have a panic attack?**

YES ____ NO ____

If YES,

b. **Other than times when you are exposed to** _______________ (specify phobic situation), **have you experienced an unexpected rush of fear/anxiety?**

YES ____ NO ____

If YES, **Where has this occurred?** ____________________________________________

If YES to 4a. or 4b., consider whether fear could be subsumed under Panic Disorder/Agoraphobia. Also consider whether the "with panic attacks" specifier should be assigned with a diagnosis of Specific Phobia (i.e., administer panic attack symptom ratings in Panic Disorder section for Other Disorder, p. 9).

5. **In what ways has this fear interfered with your life** (e.g., daily routine, job, social activities)**?; How much are you bothered by this fear?**

____________________________________________

____________________________________________

Rate interference: _______________ distress: _______________

0------------1------------2------------3------------4------------5------------6------------7------------8

None | Mild | Moderate | Severe | Very severe

6a. **When did your fear and avoidance of** _________ **become a problem?** (Determine when the Specific Phobia met *DSM-5* threshold; i.e., when the fear/avoidance of the object/situation became sufficiently prominent to cause clinically significant interference and distress.)

____________________________________________

Date of Disorder Onset: _______________ Month _______________ Year

b. **Can you recall anything that might have led to this fear?**

____________________________________________

____________________________________________

7a. **Besides this current period, have there been other, separate periods of time before this when you were bothered by this same fear** (inquire about discrete, previous episodes of Specific Phobia for this object/situation that were followed by periods of remission)?

YES ____ NO ____

b. If YES, **When did this/these past period(s) of fears and avoidance occur?**

____________________________________________

IF YES, go to INITIAL INQUIRY (PAST ratings, p. 53) and PAST EPISODES (p. 56)

## III. PAST EPISODES

Complete for each specific fear that was potentially of clinical severity:

**Now I want to ask you a series of questions about your past specific fears:**

A. Specific Fear #1: ____________________________________________

1. **What were you concerned would happen in this situation?** ______________________________

______________________________

2. **Did you feel anxious nearly every time you entered this situation or when you were faced with the possibility of having to enter this situation?**

YES ____ NO ____

3. **Did the anxiety occur as soon as you entered the situation or were about to enter the situation, or was the anxiety sometimes delayed or unexpected?**

IMMEDIATE ____ DELAYED ____

4a. **Were you anxious about these situations because you were afraid you would have a panic attack?**

YES ____ NO ____

If YES,

b. **Other than times when you were exposed to** ______________ (specify phobic situation), **did you experience an unexpected rush of fear/anxiety?**

YES ____ NO ____

If YES, **Where did that occur?** ______________________________

If YES to 4a. or 4b., consider whether fear could be subsumed under Panic Disorder/Agoraphobia. Also consider whether the "with panic attacks" specifier should be assigned with a diagnosis of Specific Phobia (i.e., administer panic attack symptom ratings in Panic Disorder section for Other Disorder, p. 9).

5. **In what ways did this fear interfere with your life** (e.g., daily routine, job, social activities)**?; How much were you bothered by this fear?**

______________________________

______________________________

Rate interference: ______________ distress: ______________

0------------1------------2------------3------------4------------5------------6------------7------------8

None Mild Moderate Severe Very severe

6a. **When did your fear and avoidance of** ________ **become a problem?** (Determine when the Specific Phobia met *DSM-5* threshold; i.e., when the fear/avoidance of the object/situation became sufficiently prominent to cause clinically significant interference and distress.)

______________________________

Date of Disorder Onset: ______________ Month ______________ Year

b. **Can you recall anything that might have led to this fear?**

YES ____ NO ____

______________________________

______________________________

7a. **When was the anxiety about** ______________ **no longer a problem in that you were comfortable with** ______________**, or it no longer caused a lot of distress or interference with your life?**

Date of Remission: ______________ Month ______________ Year

b. **Can you recall any reasons why you were no longer anxious about this object/situation?**

YES ____ NO ____

______________________________________________________________________

______________________________________________________________________

8a. **Prior to or after this period, have there been other, separate periods of time when you were bothered by this same fear** (inquire about discrete, other episodes of Specific Phobia for this object/situation that were followed by periods of remission)?

YES ____ NO ____

b. If YES, **When did this/these other period(s) of fears and avoidance occur?**

______________________________________________________________________

IF YES, go to INITIAL INQUIRY (PAST ratings, p. 53) and PAST EPISODES (p. 56).

B. Specific Fear #2: ______________________________________________________________________

1. **What were you concerned would happen in this situation?** ______________________________________________________________________

______________________________________________________________________

2. **Did you feel anxious nearly every time you entered this situation or when you were faced with the possibility of having to enter this situation?**

YES ____ NO ____

3. **Did the anxiety occur as soon as you entered the situation or were about to enter the situation, or was the anxiety sometimes delayed or unexpected?**

IMMEDIATE ____ DELAYED ____

4a. **Were you anxious about these situations because you were afraid you would have a panic attack?**

YES ____ NO ____

If YES,

b. **Other than times when you were exposed to** ______________ (specify phobic situation)**, did you experience an unexpected rush of fear/anxiety?**

YES ____ NO ____

If YES, **Where did that occur?** ______________________________________________________________________

If YES to 4a. or 4b., consider whether fear could be subsumed under Panic Disorder/Agoraphobia. Also consider whether the "with panic attacks" specifier should be assigned with a diagnosis of Specific Phobia (i.e., administer panic attack symptom ratings in Panic Disorder section for Other Disorder, p. 9).

5. **In what ways did this fear interfere with your life** (e.g., daily routine, job, social activities)?**; How much were you bothered by this fear?**

______________________________________________________________________

______________________________________________________________________

Rate interference: ______________ distress: ______________

0-----------1-----------2-----------3-----------4-----------5-----------6-----------7-----------8

None Mild Moderate Severe Very severe

6a. **When did your fear and avoidance of ________ become a problem?** (Determine when the specific phobia met *DSM-5* threshold; i.e., when the fear/avoidance of the object/situation became sufficiently prominent to cause clinically significant interference and distress.)

______________________________________________________________________________

Date of Disorder Onset: _______________ Month _______________ Year

b. **Can you recall anything that might have led to this fear?**

YES ____ NO ____

______________________________________________________________________________

______________________________________________________________________________

7a. **When was the anxiety about _______________ no longer a problem in that you were comfortable with _______________, or it no longer caused a lot of distress or interference with your life?**

Date of Remission: _______________ Month _______________ Year

b. **Can you recall any reasons why you were no longer anxious about this object/situation?**

YES ____ NO ____

______________________________________________________________________________

______________________________________________________________________________

8a. **Prior to or after this period, have there been other, separate periods of time when you were bothered by this same fear** (inquire about discrete, other episodes of Specific Phobia for this object/situation that were followed by periods of remission)?

YES ____ NO ____

b. If YES, **When did this/these other period(s) of fears and avoidance occur?**

______________________________________________________________________________

IF YES, go to INITIAL INQUIRY (PAST ratings, p. 53) and PAST EPISODES (p. 56).

IF NO, skip to POSTTRAUMATIC STRESS DISORDER (p. 60).

# POSTTRAUMATIC STRESS DISORDER/ACUTE STRESS DISORDER

## I. INITIAL INQUIRY

**I am going to describe a number of traumatic or life-threatening events, and ask you whether you experienced or witnessed any of the events during your lifetime.**

Record the dates and details of each endorsed event in the space provided below the event. For each endorsed event, indicate whether the patient experienced the event personally or witnessed the event in person as it occurred to others (or both; e.g., ongoing childhood abuse of self and siblings). In addition, indicate whether the event was associated with actual or threatened death, serious injury, and/or sexual violation. Using the scale below, rate the severity of the event (if no history of event, rate "0"); for recurring events, also consider the frequency and time span of the event in the severity rating. If the patient endorses multiple events within a given event category (e.g., multiple transportation accidents), rate the most severe event (i.e., associated with the highest threat of death/serious injury, identified by the patient as most distressing).

EXPERIENCED (EXP): Indicate with a checkmark if the patient experienced the event personally.

WITNESSED (WIT): Indicate with a checkmark if the patient witnessed the event in person as it occurred to others.

DEATH/INJURY/SEXUAL VIOLATION (D/I): Indicate with a checkmark if the event was associated with actual or threatened death, serious injury, and/or sexual violation.

EVENT SEVERITY (SEV):

0------------1------------2------------3------------4------------5------------6------------7------------8

None — Mild — Moderate — Severe — Very severe

| | EXP | WIT | D/I | SEV |
|---|---|---|---|---|
| 1. Physical abuse/assault (e.g., childhood, domestic violence)<br>________________________________________ | ___ | ___ | ___ | ___ |
| 2. Sexual abuse/assault (e.g., childhood, attempted or completed rape)<br>________________________________________ | ___ | ___ | ___ | ___ |
| 3. Transportation accident (e.g., car, plane crash)<br>________________________________________ | ___ | ___ | ___ | ___ |
| 4. Other serious accident (e.g., falls, fire)<br>________________________________________ | ___ | ___ | ___ | ___ |
| 5. Crime victimization (e.g., armed robbery, mugging, captivity)<br>________________________________________ | ___ | ___ | ___ | ___ |
| 6. Natural disaster (e.g., flood, hurricane, tornado)<br>________________________________________ | ___ | ___ | ___ | ___ |
| 7. Combat/Exposure to war-zone<br>________________________________________ | ___ | ___ | ___ | ___ |
| 8. Learning about a serious event (violent or accidental) that occurred to close relative or close friend (e.g., death of loved one due to crime victimization or accident)<br>________________________________________ | ___ | ___ | ___ | ___ |
| 9. Repeated or extreme exposure to aversive details/aftermath of violent events/accidents (e.g., repeated first responder to trauma or crime scenes)<br>________________________________________ | ___ | ___ | ___ | ___ |

EXP WIT D/I SEV

10. Other

______________________________________________ ___ ___ ___ ___

11. Other

______________________________________________ ___ ___ ___ ___

If there is any uncertainty regarding when the traumatic event(s) occurred/began, ask:

12a. **Do you recall the date the event(s) occurred/began?** (*Note*: if patient is vague in date of occurrence, attempt to ascertain more specific information, e.g., by linking onset to objective life events.)

______________________________________________

Date of Event(s): ______________ Month ______________ Year

For events that were ongoing (e.g., recurrent physical abuse), but have stopped, ask:

b. **Do you recall when the event(s) ended?**

______________________________________________

Date Event(s) Ended: ______________ Month ______________ Year

*Note*: If the trauma is still ongoing, specify in space above.

**************************************************************************************************

If no history of exposure to traumatic event(s),
Skip to **MAJOR DEPRESSIVE DISORDER** (p. 68).

**************************************************************************************************

## II. INTRUSION SYMPTOMS

1a. **Currently, are you bothered by recurrent and distressing memories, thoughts, or dreams about the event, or distress when you hear or see things that remind you of the event?**

YES ____ NO ____

If YES, skip to 2a.

b. **Since the event occurred, have you ever been bothered by recurrent and distressing memories, thoughts, or dreams about the event, or distress when you hear or see things that remind you of the event?**

YES ____ NO ____

If NO to 1a. and 1b., skip to INTRUSION SYMPTOM RATINGS.

IF YES to 1a. or 1b., ask:

2a. **How soon after the event occurred/began did you begin having these symptoms?**

______________________________________________

b. **After these symptoms began, [have/did] you experience(d) them continuously, or [have there been/were there] periods of time after the symptoms began that you were not bothered by them?** [To foster subsequent inquiry, try to begin to establish dates of onset/remission and presence of more than one discrete episodes of disturbance.]

______________________________________________

______________________________________________

A. INTRUSION SYMPTOM RATINGS

CURRENT ratings should be obtained for: (a) patients who do not report current or past intrusions; and (b) patients who report current intrusions only. If patient only reports past intrusions, initially obtain PAST ratings. In these cases, CURRENT symptom ratings should then be obtained after establishing either: (a) a past diagnosis of PTSD in the PAST EPISODE section (e.g., to determine partial/full remission); or (b) the absence of past PTSD diagnoses after administration of the PAST EPISODE section or determining the absence of clinically significant intrusions after administering PAST ratings. If there is evidence of separate episodes, inquire about the presence of discrete episodes of disturbance (e.g., "**Since the symptom began, have there been periods of time when you were not bothered by it?**"). For patients endorsing both current and past episodes, CURRENT ratings should be obtained first and PAST ratings should be obtained after completing the CURRENT EPISODE section. Use the space below each symptom to record the specific nature of that symptom (e.g., cues that elicit distress associated with the trauma). If it is determined that a symptom can be better accounted for by another disorder, rate it "0." Use Comments section to record clinically useful information (e.g., data pertaining to discreteness of episodes, duration of symptom more consistent with Acute Stress Disorder). Note that symptom ratings can be made in association with multiple traumatic events, if present.

For each intrusion symptom, make ratings of Recurrence/Distress (i.e., frequency and intensity) using the scale and suggested queries below.

RECURRENCE/DISTRESS:

**How often [do/did] you experience _______________ ?; How much distress [does/did] this produce?**

0------------1------------2------------3------------4------------5------------6------------7------------8

| 0 | 2 | 4 | 6 | 8 |
|---|---|---|---|---|
| Never/ No distress | Rarely/Mild distress | Occasionally/ Moderate distress | Frequently/ Marked distress | Constantly/ Extreme distress |

| | CURRENT | PAST | COMMENTS |
|---|---|---|---|
| 1. Recurrent, intrusive recollections of the event (e.g., images, thoughts, perceptions) ______________________________ | ___ | ___ | ______________________ |
| 2. Recurrent distressing dreams or nightmares of the event ______________________________ | ___ | ___ | ______________________ |
| 3. Acting or feeling as if the event were recurring (e.g., flashbacks, hallucinations, illusions, reliving the trauma) ______________________________ | ___ | ___ | ______________________ |
| 4. Emotional distress at exposure to internal or external cues that are reminders of the event ______________________________ | ___ | ___ | ______________________ |
| 5. Physical symptom reactions to internal or external cues that are reminders of the event ______________________________ | ___ | ___ | ______________________ |

**************************************************************************************************

If no evidence of one or more current or past intrusion symptoms,
Skip to **MAJOR DEPRESSIVE DISORDER** (p. 68).

**************************************************************************************************

## III. CURRENT EPISODE

If evidence of a discrete past episode, preface inquiry in this section with: **Now I want to ask you a series of questions about this current period when you have been experiencing recurrent and distressing memories/dreams/thoughts of the event(s), beginning roughly in ______________** (specify dates).

Specify traumatic event(s): ______________________________________________

A. SYMPTOM RATINGS

SEVERITY: **Since the event(s) occurred/began, how often have you experienced ______________?; How distressing/severe has this symptom been for you?** (Do not record symptoms better accounted for by other conditions such as panic, depression, and generalized anxiety disorder.)

0------------1------------2------------3------------4------------5------------6------------7------------8

| 0 | 2 | 4 | 6 | 8 |
|---|---|---|---|---|
| Never/ None | Rarely/Mild | Occasionally/ Moderate | Frequently/ Severe | Constantly/ Very severe |

BEGIN/WORSEN (BEG): **Did this symptom begin or worsen after the event(s) occurred/began?**

| | SEVERITY | BEG |
|---|---|---|
| Avoidance of Associated Stimuli | | |
| 1. Avoidance of, or efforts to avoid, distressing memories, thoughts, or feelings associated with the event(s) | ___ | Y N |
| 2. Avoidance of, or efforts to avoid, external reminders (e.g. people, places, activities, objects, situations) that trigger distressing memories, thoughts, or feelings of the event(s) | ___ | Y N |
| Negative Alterations in Cognitions or Mood | | |
| 3. Inability to recall important aspect of the event | ___ | Y N |
| 4. Strong negative beliefs about oneself, others, or the world | ___ | Y N |
| 5. Blame of self or others about cause or consequences of the event(s) | ___ | Y N |
| 6. Chronic negative emotional state (e.g., fear, horror, anger, guilt, shame) | ___ | Y N |
| 7. Decreased interest or participation in significant activities | ___ | Y N |
| 8. Feeling detached or emotionally distant from others | ___ | Y N |
| 9. Inability to experience positive emotions (e.g., happiness, satisfaction, loving feelings) | ___ | Y N |
| Hyperarousal/Hyperreactivity | | |
| 10. Irritable behavior and angry outbursts (e.g., verbal or physical aggression toward people objects with little/no provocation) | ___ | Y N |
| 11. Reckless or self-destructive behavior | ___ | Y N |
| 12. Hypervigilance (e.g., constant vigilance of surroundings) | ___ | Y N |
| 13. Exaggerated startle response | ___ | Y N |
| 14. Difficulty concentrating | ___ | Y N |
| 15. Difficulty falling or staying asleep; restless sleep | ___ | Y N |
| Depersonalization/Derealization (Dissociative Symptoms specifier) | | |
| 16. Feeling detached from oneself or one's thoughts (e.g., feeling in a dream-like state, outside observer of oneself, time moving slowly) | ___ | Y N |
| 17. Feelings of unreality of surroundings (e.g., world is experienced as unreal, dreamlike, distant, or distorted) | ___ | Y N |

B. INTERFERENCE/ONSET

1. **In what ways have these recurrent and distressing memories/thoughts/dreams and the symptoms associated with them interfered with your life** (e.g., daily routine, job, social activities)**?; How much are you bothered by these symptoms?**

_______________

_______________

Rate interference: _______________ distress: _______________

0------------1------------2------------3------------4------------5------------6------------7------------8

None Mild Moderate Severe Very severe

If there is any uncertainty regarding the onset of the disorder, ask:

2a. **When did your recurrent and distressing memories/thoughts/dreams and the symptoms associated with them become a problem?** (Determine when the PTSD symptoms met *DSM-5* threshold; i.e., when a sufficient number of clinically significant symptoms were present in each of the *DSM-5* symptom clusters.)

_______________

Date of Disorder Onset: _______________ Month _______________ Year

b. If uncertain, ask: **How soon after the event occurred/began did you begin having the recurrent and distressing memories/thoughts/dreams as well as the other symptoms associated with them?**

_______________

*Note*: Assign PTSD with Delayed Expression if the symptoms did not meet the *DSM-5* diagnostic threshold until at least 6 months after the event. If symptoms have lasted four weeks or less, consider Acute Stress Disorder.

3. **Have you been regularly taking any types of drugs or medications during this current period when you've had these recurrent and distressing memories/thoughts/dreams and associated symptoms?**

YES ____ NO ____

Specify (type; amount; dates of use): _______________

_______________

4. **At the time of or since these symptoms began, did you have any physical condition** (e.g., seizures)**?**

YES ____ NO ____

Specify (type; date of onset/remission): _______________

_______________

5a. **Besides this current period of time when you've had these recurrent and distressing memories/thoughts/dreams, have there been other, separate periods of time before this when you have had the same problems either in relation to this event(s) or to another event(s)** (inquire about discrete, previous episodes of Posttraumatic Stress Disorder that were followed by periods of remission)**?**

YES ____ NO ____

b. If YES, **When did this/these past period(s) of recurrent memories/thoughts/dreams occur?**

_______________

IF YES, go to INTRUSION SYMPTOM RATINGS, PAST (p. 62). If there is evidence of an additional traumatic event, record the nature and dates of this event in INITIAL INQUIRY.

If NO, skip to MAJOR DEPRESSIVE DISORDER (p. 68).

## IV. PAST EPISODE

**Now I want to ask you a series of questions about the past period when you had been experiencing recurrent and distressing memories/dreams/thoughts of the event that began roughly in ______________ and ended roughly in** ______________ (specify dates).

Specify traumatic event(s): ______________________________________________

A. SYMPTOM RATINGS

SEVERITY: **Since the event(s) occurred/began, how often did you experience ______________?; How distressing/severe was this symptom for you?** (Do not record symptoms better accounted for by other conditions such as panic, depression, and generalized anxiety disorder.)

| 0 | 1 | 2 | 3 | 4 | 5 | 6 | 7 | 8 |
|---|---|---|---|---|---|---|---|---|
| Never/ None | | Rarely/Mild | | Occasionally/ Moderate | | Frequently/ Severe | | Constantly/ Very severe |

BEGIN/WORSEN (BEG): **Did this symptom begin or worsen after the event(s) occurred/began?**

| | SEVERITY | BEG |
|---|---|---|
| Avoidance of Associated Stimuli | | |
| 1. Avoidance of, or efforts to avoid, distressing memories, thoughts, or feelings associated with the event(s) | ___ | Y N |
| 2. Avoidance of, or efforts to avoid, external reminders (e.g. people, places, activities, objects, situations) that trigger distressing memories, thoughts, or feelings of the event(s) | ___ | Y N |
| Negative Alterations in Cognitions or Mood | | |
| 3. Inability to recall important aspect of the event | ___ | Y N |
| 4. Strong negative beliefs about oneself, others, or the world | ___ | Y N |
| 5. Blame of self or others about cause or consequences of the event(s) | ___ | Y N |
| 6. Chronic negative emotional state (e.g., fear, horror, anger, guilt, shame) | ___ | Y N |
| 7. Decreased interest or participation in significant activities | ___ | Y N |
| 8. Feeling detached or emotionally distant from others | ___ | Y N |
| 9. Inability to experience positive emotions (e.g., happiness, satisfaction, loving feelings) | ___ | Y N |
| Hyperarousal/Hyperreactivity | | |
| 10. Irritable behavior and angry outbursts (e.g., verbal or physical aggression toward people objects with little/no provocation) | ___ | Y N |
| 11. Reckless or self-destructive behavior | ___ | Y N |
| 12. Hypervigilance (e.g., constant vigilance of surroundings) | ___ | Y N |
| 13. Exaggerated startle response | ___ | Y N |
| 14. Difficulty concentrating | ___ | Y N |
| 15. Difficulty falling or staying asleep; restless sleep | ___ | Y N |
| Depersonalization/Derealization (Dissociative Symptoms specifier) | | |
| 16. Feeling detached from oneself or one's thoughts (e.g., feeling in a dream-like state, outside observer of oneself, time moving slowly) | ___ | Y N |
| 17. Feelings of unreality of surroundings (e.g., world is experienced as unreal, dreamlike, distant, or distorted) | ___ | Y N |

B. INTERFERENCE/ONSET

1. **In what ways did these recurrent and distressing memories/thoughts/dreams and the symptoms associated with them interfere with your life** (e.g., daily routine, job, social activities)**?; How much were you bothered by these symptoms?**

______________________________________________________________________

______________________________________________________________________

Rate interference: ______________ distress: ______________

0------------1------------2------------3------------4------------5------------6------------7------------8

None Mild Moderate Severe Very severe

If there is any uncertainty regarding the onset of the disorder, ask:

2a. **During that time, when did your recurrent and distressing memories/thoughts/dreams and the symptoms associated with them become a problem?** (Determine when the PTSD symptoms met *DSM-5* threshold; i.e., when a sufficient number of clinically significant symptoms were present in each of the *DSM-5* symptom clusters.)

______________________________________________________________________

Date of Disorder Onset: ______________ Month ______________ Year

b. If uncertain, ask: **How soon after the event occurred/began did you begin having the recurrent and distressing memories/thoughts/dreams as well as the other symptoms associated with them?**

______________________________________________________________________

*Note*: Assign PTSD with Delayed Expression if the symptoms did not meet the *DSM-5* diagnostic threshold until at least 6 months after the event. If symptoms lasted no longer than four weeks, consider Acute Stress Disorder.

3. **During that past period of time when you were having these recurrent and distressing memories/thoughts/dreams and associated symptoms, were you regularly taking any types of drugs or medications?**

YES ____ NO ____

Specify (type; amount; dates of use): ______________________________________________

______________________________________________________________________

4. **At the time of or since these symptoms began, did you have any physical condition** (e.g., seizures)**?**

YES ____ NO ____

Specify (type; date of onset/remission): ______________________________________________

______________________________________________________________________

5a. **When was this no longer a problem, in that the memories/thoughts/dreams did not occur persistently, you weren't bothered by them, and these memories and the symptoms associated with them did not interfere with your life?**

Date of remission: ______________ Month ______________ Year

b. **Can you recall any reasons why these symptoms subsided?**

YES ____ NO ____

______________________________________________________________________

______________________________________________________________________

6a. **Prior to or after this period of recurrent and distressing memories/thoughts/dreams, have there been other, separate periods of time that we haven't covered when you have had the same problems either in relation to this event(s) or to another event(s)?** (inquire about discrete, other episodes of Posttraumatic Stress Disorder that were followed by periods of remission)**?**

YES ____ NO ____

b. If YES, **When did this/these other period(s) of recurrent memories/thoughts/dreams occur?**

________________________________________

IF YES, go to INTRUSION SYMPTOM RATINGS, PAST (p. 62). If there is evidence of an additional traumatic event, record the nature and dates of this event in INITIAL INQUIRY (p. 60).

If NO, go back to INTRUSION SYMPTOM RATINGS to obtain CURRENT ratings (also obtain CURRENT ratings in other symptom clusters if a past PTSD diagnosis is present); then skip to MAJOR DEPRESSIVE DISORDER (p. 68).

# MAJOR DEPRESSIVE DISORDER

## I. INITIAL INQUIRY

1a. **Currently, have you been feeling depressed, sad, empty, or hopeless?**

YES ____ NO ____

b. **Currently, have you lost interest or pleasure in almost all of your usual activities?**

YES ____ NO ____

c. **Currently, have other people commented to you that you appear down or tearful or that you seem less interested in your usual activities?**

YES ____ NO ____

If YES to either 1a., 1b., or 1c., skip to 2a.

If NO to 1a., 1b., and 1c., continue to 1d.

d. **Have you ever experienced a period of two weeks or more when you felt depressed, empty, hopeless, or lost interest or pleasure in your usual activities?**

YES ____ NO ____

IF NO to 1a. through 1d., skip to SYMPTOM RATINGS

IF YES to 1a., 1b., 1c., or 1d., ask:

2a. **When did these symptoms first begin?** ______________________________

b. **After these symptoms began, [have/did] you experience(d) them continuously, or [have there been/were there] periods of time after the symptoms began that you were not bothered by them?** [To foster subsequent inquiry, try to begin to establish dates of onset/remission and presence of more than one discrete episodes of disturbance.]

______________________________

______________________________

If evidence of more than one depressive episode, ask:

c. **What would you identify as the period of time when you experienced the feelings of depression/ loss of interest in usual activities at their worst or most severe levels?**

______________________________

______________________________

## II. SYMPTOM RATINGS

CURRENT symptom ratings should be obtained for: (a) patients who do not report depression (or loss of interest); and (b) patients who report current depression only. If patient only reports past depression, initially obtain PAST symptom ratings. In these cases, CURRENT symptom ratings should be obtained after establishing either: (a) a past diagnosis of Major Depressive Disorder in the PAST EPISODE sections (e.g., to determine partial/full remission); or (b) the absence of past Major Depressive Disorder diagnoses after administration of a PAST EPISODE section or determining the absence of clinically significant depressive symptoms after administering PAST symptom ratings. If there is evidence of separate episodes, inquire about the presence of discrete episodes of disturbance (e.g., "**Since these symptoms began, have there been periods of time when you were not bothered by them?**"). For patients endorsing both current and past episodes, CURRENT symptom ratings should be obtained first and PAST ratings should be obtained after completing the CURRENT

EPISODE section. If it is determined a symptom can be subsumed by another disorder, rate it "0." Record symptoms that are present during the same two-week period and represent a change from previous functioning.

PAST EPISODES: Obtain symptom ratings for the first major depressive episode under the PAST #1 column. If there are two past depressive episodes, rate the second episode under the PAST #2 column. If there are more than two past depressive episodes, either: (a) rate the worst episode under the PAST #2 column, if the worst episode is not the first or current episode, or (b) rate the most recent past episode under the PAST #2 column, if the worst episode is the first or current episode.

CURRENT: **Over the past 2 weeks, have you experienced ______________?;**
**Have you experienced ______________ nearly every day over the past 2 weeks?**

PAST: **During that period of time in** __________ (dates), **did you experience ______________ ?;**
**Did you experience ______________ nearly every day for a period of 2 weeks or more?**

SEVERITY (SEV):

0------------1------------2------------3------------4------------5------------6------------7------------8
None — Mild — Moderate — Severe — Very severe

NEARLY EVERY DAY (DAY): Indicate Yes or No

| | CURRENT | | PAST #1 (FIRST) | | PAST #2 (SECOND/WORST) | |
|---|---|---|---|---|---|---|
| | SEV | DAY | SEV | DAY | SEV | DAY |
| 1. Depressed mood (e.g., sad, empty, hopeless, tearful) | ___ | Y N | ___ | Y N | ___ | Y N |
| 2. Loss of interest and pleasure in usual activities | ___ | Y N | ___ | Y N | ___ | Y N |
| 3. Weight/appetite change (either a. or b.) | | | | | | |
| a. Significant weight loss (≥ 5% drop in a month) or decrease in appetite | ___ | Y N | ___ | Y N | ___ | Y N |
| b. Significant weight gain (≥ 5% gain in a month) or increase in appetite | ___ | Y N | ___ | Y N | ___ | Y N |
| 4. Sleep disturbance (either a. or b.) | | | | | | |
| a. Insomnia | ___ | Y N | ___ | Y N | ___ | Y N |
| b. Hypersomnia | ___ | Y N | ___ | Y N | ___ | Y N |
| 5. Motor disturbance (either a. or b.) | | | | | | |
| a. Psychomotor agitation; **Unable to sit still?** (must be observable) | ___ | Y N | ___ | Y N | ___ | Y N |
| b. Psychomotor retardation; **[Feel/Felt] so slowed down that it [is/was] hard to move or carry on a conversation?** (must be observable) | ___ | Y N | ___ | Y N | ___ | Y N |
| 6. Fatigue or loss of energy | ___ | Y N | ___ | Y N | ___ | Y N |
| 7. Worthlessness, or excessive, inappropriate guilt; **[Do/Did] you blame yourself for anything or feel guilty?** | ___ | Y N | ___ | Y N | ___ | Y N |
| 8. Impaired concentration, slowed thinking, or indecisiveness; **Thinking slowed down, or hard to make decisions?** | ___ | Y N | ___ | Y N | ___ | Y N |
| 9. Thoughts of death or suicide; **Think about death or hurting yourself? How much [do/did] you think about it?** | ___ | Y N | ___ | Y N | ___ | Y N |

If YES to 9., inquire about the extent of suicidal ideation or intent (e.g., history of prior attempts, presence/extent of current plan, access to method for carrying out plan, ability to state reasons for living):

CURRENT: ____________________

PAST #1: ____________________

PAST #2: ____________________

*****************************************************************************************************

If no evidence of clinically significant major depressive symptoms,
Skip to **PERSISTENT DEPRESSIVE DISORDER** (p. 75).

*****************************************************************************************************

## III. CURRENT EPISODE

If evidence of a discrete past episode(s), preface inquiry in this section with: **Now I want to ask you a series of questions about this <u>current</u> period of time when you felt depressed/loss of interest that began roughly in** ______________ (specify dates).

1. **In what ways have these symptoms of depression interfered with your life** (e.g., daily routine, job, social activities)**?; How much are you bothered about having these symptoms?**

____________________

____________________

Rate interference: ______________ distress: ______________

0------------1------------2------------3------------4------------5------------6------------7------------8

None　　Mild　　Moderate　　Severe　　Very severe

2a. **When did your depressed mood and symptoms accompanying the depression become a problem?** (Determine when the major depression met *DSM-5* threshold; i.e., when the depressed mood, loss of interest, and associated symptoms became sufficient in number and severity to cause clinically significant interference and distress.)

____________________

Date of Disorder Onset: ______________ Month ______________ Year

*Note*: Consider a diagnosis of Persistent Depressive Disorder if duration has been longer than 2 years.

b. **Can you recall anything that might have led to this problem?**

YES ____ NO ____

____________________

____________________

c. **Were you under any type of stress during this time?**

YES ____ NO ____

**What was happening in your life at the time?**

____________________

____________________

3. **Have you been regularly taking any types of drugs or medications during this current period of depression** (include drugs of abuse, medication)**?**

YES ____ NO ____

Specify (type; amount; dates of use): ______________________________

______________________________

4. **At the time of or since these symptoms began, did you have any physical condition** (e.g., pregnancy, hypothyroidism, hypoglycemia)**?**

YES ____ NO ____

Specify (type; date of onset/remission): ______________________________

______________________________

5a. **Besides this current period of depression and/or loss of interest in usual activities, have there been other, separate periods of time before this when you had these symptoms** (inquire about discrete, previous episodes of Major Depressive Disorder that were followed by periods of remission)**?**

YES ____ NO ____

b. If YES, **When did this/these past period(s) of depression/loss of interest occur?**

______________________________

If YES, go back to SYMPTOM RATINGS, PAST (p. 69).

If NO, skip to PERSISTENT DEPRESSIVE DISORDER (p. 75)

## IV. PAST EPISODE: FIRST EPISODE

**Now I want to ask you a series of questions about the past period of depression/loss of interest that began roughly in ______________ and ended roughly in ______________** (specify dates).

1. **In what ways did the symptoms of depression interfere with your life** (e.g., daily routine, job, social activities)**?; How much were you bothered about having these symptoms?**

______________________________

______________________________

Rate interference: ______________ distress: ______________

0------------1------------2------------3------------4------------5------------6------------7------------8

None Mild Moderate Severe Very severe

2a. **During that time, when did your depressed mood and symptoms accompanying the depression become a problem?** (Determine when the major depression met *DSM-5* threshold; i.e., when the depressed mood, loss of interest, and associated symptoms became sufficient in number and severity to cause clinically significant interference and distress.)

______________________________

Date of Disorder Onset: ______________ Month ______________ Year

b. **Can you recall anything that might have led to this problem?**

YES ____ NO ____

______________________________

______________________________

c. **Were you under any type of stress during this time?**

YES ____ NO ____

**What was happening in your life at the time?**

______________________________________________________________________

______________________________________________________________________

3. **During that period of depression, were you regularly taking any types of drugs or medications** (include drugs of abuse, medication)**?**

YES ____ NO ____

Specify (type; amount; dates of use): ______________________________________________

______________________________________________________________________

4. **At the time of or since the symptoms began, did you have any physical condition** (e.g., pregnancy, hypothyroidism, hypoglycemia)**?**

YES ____ NO ____

Specify (type; date of onset/remission): ______________________________________________

______________________________________________________________________

5a. **When was the depression and symptoms accompanying the depression no longer a problem, in that they no longer occurred persistently, you were not bothered by these symptoms, and they did not interfere with your life?**

Date of remission: ______________ Month ______________ Year

*Note*: Consider a diagnosis of Persistent Depressive Disorder if duration was longer than 2 years.

b. **Can you recall any reasons why these feelings of depression were no longer a problem for you?**

YES ____ NO ____

______________________________________________________________________

______________________________________________________________________

6a. **Prior to or after this past period of depression and/or loss of interest in usual activities, have there been other, separate periods of time that we haven't covered when you have had the same problems** (inquire about discrete, other episodes of Major Depressive Disorder that were followed by periods of remission)**?**

YES ____ NO ____

b. If YES, **When did this/these other period(s) of depression occur?**

______________________________________________________________________

If YES, go back to SYMPTOM RATINGS, PAST (p. 69).

If NO, go back to SYMPTOM RATINGS to obtain CURRENT ratings (p. 69); administer SPECIFIERS (p. 74), if necessary; then skip to PERSISTENT DEPRESSIVE DISORDER (p. 75).

## V. PAST EPISODE: WORST/SECOND EPISODE

Indicate episode of inquiry (e.g., worst, most recent): ______________________________________

**Now I want to ask you a series of questions about the past period of depression/loss of interest that began roughly in ______________ and ended roughly in ______________** (specify dates).

1. **In what ways did the symptoms of depression interfere with your life** (e.g., daily routine, job, social activities)**?; How much were you bothered about having these symptoms?**

______________________________________________________________________

______________________________________________________________________

Rate interference: _______________ distress: _______________

0------------1------------2------------3------------4------------5------------6------------7------------8

None Mild Moderate Severe Very severe

2a. **During that time, when did your depressed mood and symptoms accompanying the depression become a problem?** (Determine when the major depression met *DSM-5* threshold; i.e., when the depressed mood, loss of interest, and associated symptoms became sufficient in number and severity to cause clinically significant interference and distress.)

______________________________________________________________________

Date of Disorder Onset: _______________ Month _______________ Year

b. **Can you recall anything that might have led to this problem?**

YES ____ NO ____

______________________________________________________________________

______________________________________________________________________

c. **Were you under any type of stress during this time?**

YES ____ NO ____

**What was happening in your life at the time?**

______________________________________________________________________

______________________________________________________________________

3. **During that period of depression, were you regularly taking any types of drugs or medications** (include drugs of abuse, medication)**?**

YES ____ NO ____

Specify (type; amount; dates of use): ______________________________________________

______________________________________________________________________

4. **At the time of or since the symptoms began, did you have any physical condition** (e.g., pregnancy, hypothyroidism, hypoglycemia)**?**

YES ____ NO ____

Specify (type; date of onset/remission): ______________________________________________

______________________________________________________________________

5a. **When was the depression and symptoms accompanying the depression no longer a problem, in that they no longer occurred persistently, you were not bothered by these symptoms, and they did not interfere with your life?**

Date of remission: _______________ Month _______________ Year

*Note*: Consider a diagnosis of Persistent Depressive Disorder if duration was longer than 2 years.

b. **Can you recall any reasons why these feelings of depression were no longer a problem for you?**

YES ____ NO ____

______________________________________________________________________

______________________________________________________________________

6a. **Prior to or after this past period of depression and/or loss of interest in usual activities, have there been other, separate periods of time that we haven't covered when you have had the same problems** (inquire about discrete, other episodes of Major Depressive Disorder that were followed by periods of remission)?

YES ____ NO ____

b. If YES, **When did this/these other period(s) of depression occur?**

______________________________________________

If YES, consider rating additional past episodes (go back to SYMPTOM RATINGS, PAST, p. 69).

If NO, go back to SYMPTOM RATINGS to obtain CURRENT ratings (p. 69), administer SPECIFIERS (p. 74), if necessary; then skip to PERSISTENT DEPRESSIVE DISORDER (p. 75).

## VI. SPECIFIERS

*Note*: Use this section to obtain ratings necessary to assign Depressive Disorder specifiers for symptoms not rated in the Major Depressive Disorder, Persistent Depressive Disorder, and Bipolar/Cyclothymia diagnostic sections.

**[Has/Was] this period of depression [been] accompanied by any of the following symptoms?**
**Did you experience this symptom the majority of days during this period of depression?**

SEVERITY (SEV):

0------------1------------2------------3------------4------------5------------6------------7------------8

None | Mild | Moderate | Severe | Very severe

NEARLY EVERY DAY (DAY): Indicate Yes or No

| | CURRENT | | PAST #1 (FIRST) | | PAST #2 (SECOND/WORST) | |
|---|---|---|---|---|---|---|
| | SEV | DAY | SEV | DAY | SEV | DAY |
| Anxious Distress | | | | | | |
| 1. Feeling keyed up or tense | ___ | Y N | ___ | Y N | ___ | Y N |
| 2. Feeling unusually restless | ___ | Y N | ___ | Y N | ___ | Y N |
| 3. Difficulty concentrating because of worry | ___ | Y N | ___ | Y N | ___ | Y N |
| 4. Fear that something awful may happen | ___ | Y N | ___ | Y N | ___ | Y N |
| 5. Feeling you might lose control of yourself | ___ | Y N | ___ | Y N | ___ | Y N |
| Melancholic/Atypical features | | | | | | |
| 6. (Un)reactive to pleasant stimuli (e.g., does/does not feel better when something good happens) If present, indicate whether mood is: Reactive or Unreactive (circle one) | ___ | Y N | ___ | Y N | ___ | Y N |
| 7. Depression worse in the morning | ___ | Y N | ___ | Y N | ___ | Y N |
| 8. Early morning awakening (at least 2 hours before intended) | ___ | Y N | ___ | Y N | ___ | Y N |
| 9. Overly sensitive to rejection from others (must result in social/occupational impairment) | ___ | Y N | ___ | Y N | ___ | Y N |

## PERSISTENT DEPRESSIVE DISORDER (DYSTHYMIA)

### I. INITIAL INQUIRY

1a. **Over the past 2 years, have you frequently had days where you felt down, blue, or depressed for most of the day?**

YES ____ NO ____

b. **Over the past 2 years, have other people commented to you that you often appear down, blue, or depressed?**

YES ____ NO ____

If YES to either 1a. or 1b., skip to 2a.

If NO to 1a. and 1b., continue to 1c.

c. **Have you ever experienced a period when you felt down, blue, or depressed, more days than not for 2 years or more?**

YES ____ NO ____

****************************************************************************************************

If YES to either 1a., 1b., or 1c., or uncertain, continue inquiry.
Otherwise skip to **BIPOLAR/CYCLOTHYMIA** (p. 81).

****************************************************************************************************

2a. **When did these symptoms first begin?** ______________________________

b. **After these symptoms began, [have/did] you experience(d) them continuously, or [have there been/were there] periods of time after the symptoms began that you were not bothered by them?** [To foster subsequent inquiry, try to begin to establish dates of onset/remission and presence of more than one discrete episodes of disturbance.]

______________________________

______________________________

### II. SYMPTOM RATINGS

CURRENT symptom ratings should be obtained for patients who report current depression only. If patient only reports past depression, initially obtain PAST symptom ratings. In these cases, CURRENT symptom ratings should be obtained after establishing a past diagnosis of Persistent Depressive Disorder in the PAST EPISODE section (e.g., to determine partial/full remission). If there is evidence of separate episodes, inquire about the presence of discrete episodes of disturbance (e.g., "**Since these symptoms began, have there been periods of time when you were not bothered by them?**"). For patients endorsing both current and past episodes, CURRENT symptom ratings should be obtained first and PAST ratings should be obtained after completing the CURRENT EPISODE section. If it is determined a symptom can be subsumed by another disorder, rate it "0."

CURRENT: **Over the past 2 years, have you often experienced ______________?;**
**Have you experienced ______________ more days than not over the past 2 years?**
**Was there a period of 2 months or more during this time when this symptom was absent?**

PAST: **During that period of time in** __________ (dates), **did you often experience __________?;**
**Did you experience ______________ more days than not for a period of 2 years or more?**
**Was there a period of 2 months or more during this time when this symptom was absent?**

SEVERITY (SEV):

0------------1------------2------------3------------4------------5------------6------------7------------8

None | Mild | Moderate | Severe | Very severe

PERSISTENT (PER): Indicate Yes or No

| | CURRENT | | PAST | |
|---|---|---|---|---|
| | SEV | PER | SEV | PER |
| 1. Depressed mood | ___ | Y N | ___ | Y N |
| 2. Appetite disturbance (either a. or b.) | | | | |
| a. Poor appetite | ___ | Y N | ___ | Y N |
| b. Overeating | ___ | Y N | ___ | Y N |
| 3. Sleep disturbance (either a. or b.) | | | | |
| a. Insomnia; **Have trouble sleeping, or…** | ___ | Y N | ___ | Y N |
| b. Hypersomnia; **…sleeping too much?** | ___ | Y N | ___ | Y N |
| 4. Low energy or fatigue; **Tired all the time?** | ___ | Y N | ___ | Y N |
| 5. Low self-esteem; **Down on yourself, feeling like a failure?** | ___ | Y N | ___ | Y N |
| 6. Poor concentration or difficulty making decisions | ___ | Y N | ___ | Y N |
| 7. Feelings of hopelessness; **Feeling pessimistic about the future?** | ___ | Y N | ___ | Y N |

*************************************************************************************

If no evidence of clinically significant and chronic depressive symptoms,
Skip to **BIPOLAR/CYCLOTHYMIA** (p. 81).

*************************************************************************************

## III. CURRENT EPISODE

If evidence of a discrete past episode, preface inquiry in this section with: **Now I want to ask you some more questions about this current period of time when you felt down or depressed that began roughly in** ______________ (specify dates).

1. **What percentage of the days over the past 2 years have you experienced a depressed mood for most of the day?**

   _______ %

   If uncertain, **Have you felt this way more days than not over the past 2 years?**

   YES ____ NO ____

2. **Over the past 2 years, have you had periods of 2 months or more when your mood was normal?**

   YES ____ NO ____

   If YES, **When?** FROM ______________ TO ______________

3. **In what ways have these symptoms of depression interfered with your life** (e.g., daily routine, job, social activities)**?; How much are you bothered about having these symptoms?**

________________________________________________________________

________________________________________________________________

Rate interference: ______________ distress: ______________

0------------1------------2------------3------------4------------5------------6------------7------------8

None Mild Moderate Severe Very severe

4a. **When did your depressed mood and symptoms accompanying the depression become a problem?** (Determine when the Persistent Depressive Disorder met *DSM-5* threshold; i.e., when the depressed mood and associated symptoms became sufficient in number, severity, and duration.)

________________________________________________________________

Date of Disorder Onset: ______________ Month ______________ Year

b. **Can you recall anything that might have led to this problem?**

YES ____ NO ____

________________________________________________________________

________________________________________________________________

c. **Were you under any type of stress during this time?**

YES ____ NO ____

**What was happening in your life at the time?**

________________________________________________________________

________________________________________________________________

5. **Have you been regularly taking any types of drugs or medications during this current period of depression** (include drugs of abuse, medication)**?**

YES ____ NO ____

Specify (type; amount; dates of use): ________________________________________

________________________________________________________________

6. **At the time of or since these symptoms began, did you have any physical condition** (e.g., pregnancy, hypothyroidism, hypoglycemia)**?**

YES ____ NO ____

Specify (type; date of onset/remission): ________________________________________

________________________________________________________________

7a. **Besides this current period of depression, have there been other, separate periods of time before this when you felt down or depressed more days than not for a period of two years or more** (inquire about discrete, previous episodes of Persistent Depressive Disorder that were followed by periods of remission)**?**

YES ____ NO ____

b. If YES, **When did this/these past period(s) of depression occur?**

________________________________________________________________

If YES, go back to SYMPTOM RATINGS, PAST (p. 76).

If NO, administer SPECIFIERS (p. 79), if necessary; then skip to BIPOLAR/CYCLOTHYMIA (p. 81).

## IV. PAST EPISODE

**Now I want to ask you a series of questions about the past period of depression that began roughly in _______________ and ended roughly in _______________** (specify dates).

1. **During that period of time in _______________** (dates)**, on average, what percentage of the days did you experience a depressed mood for most of the day?**

   _______ %

   If uncertain, **On average, did you feel this way more days than not during this period (of 2 years or more?**

   YES ____ NO ____

2. **During that period, did you have periods of 2 months or more when your mood was normal?**

   YES ____ NO ____

   If YES, **When?** FROM _______________ TO _______________

3. **In what ways did these symptoms of depression interfere with your life** (e.g., daily routine, job, social activities)**?; How much were you bothered about having these symptoms?**

   ______________________________________________________________________

   ______________________________________________________________________

   Rate interference: _______________ distress: _______________

   0------------1------------2------------3------------4------------5------------6------------7------------8

   None Mild Moderate Severe Very severe

4a. **During that time, when did your depressed mood and symptoms accompanying the depression become a problem?** (Determine when the Persistent Depressive Disorder met *DSM-5* threshold; i.e., when the depressed mood and associated symptoms became sufficient in number, severity, and duration.)

   ______________________________________________________________________

   Date of Disorder Onset: _______________ Month _______________ Year

b. **Can you recall anything that might have led to this problem?**

   YES ____ NO ____

   ______________________________________________________________________

   ______________________________________________________________________

c. **Were you under any type of stress during this time?**

   YES ____ NO ____

   **What was happening in your life at the time?**

   ______________________________________________________________________

   ______________________________________________________________________

5. **During that period of depression, were you regularly taking any types of drugs or medications** (include drugs of abuse, medication)?

   YES ____ NO ____

   Specify (type; amount; dates of use): ______________________________________________

   ______________________________________________________________________

6. **At the time of or since the symptoms began, did you have any physical condition** (e.g., pregnancy, hypothyroidism, hypoglycemia)**?**

YES ____ NO ____

Specify (type; date of onset/remission): ________________________________________

________________________________________

7a. **When was the depression and symptoms accompanying the depression no longer a problem, in that they no longer occurred persistently, you were not bothered by these symptoms, and they did not interfere with your life?**

Date of remission: ______________ Month ______________ Year

b. **Can you recall any reasons why these feelings of depression were no longer a problem for you?**

YES ____ NO ____

________________________________________

________________________________________

8a. **Prior to or after this past period of depression, have there been other, separate periods of time that we haven't covered when you have had the same problems** (inquire about discrete, other episodes of Persistent Depressive Disorder that were followed by periods of remission)**?**

YES ____ NO ____

b. If YES, **When did this/these other period(s) of depression occur?**

________________________________________

If YES, go back to SYMPTOM RATINGS, PAST (p. 76).

If NO, go back to SYMPTOM RATINGS to obtain CURRENT ratings (p. 76); administer SPECIFIERS (p. 79), if necessary; then skip to BIPOLAR/CYCLOTHYMIA (p. 81).

## V. SPECIFIERS

*Note*: Use this section to obtain ratings necessary to assign Depressive Disorder specifiers for symptoms not rated in the Major Depressive Disorder, Persistent Depressive Disorder, and Bipolar/Cyclothymia diagnostic sections.

**[Has/Was] this period of depression [been] accompanied by any of the following symptoms?**
**Did you experience this symptom the majority of days during this period of depression?**

SEVERITY (SEV):

0------------1------------2------------3------------4------------5------------6------------7------------8

None Mild Moderate Severe Very severe

NEARLY EVERY DAY (DAY): Indicate Yes or No

| | CURRENT | | PAST | |
|---|---|---|---|---|
| | SEV | DAY | SEV | DAY |
| Anxious Distress | | | | |
| 1. Feeling keyed up or tense | ___ | Y N | ___ | Y N |
| 2. Feeling unusually restless | ___ | Y N | ___ | Y N |

0------------1------------2------------3------------4------------5------------6------------7------------8

None | Mild | Moderate | Severe | Very severe

| | CURRENT | | PAST | |
|---|---|---|---|---|
| | SEV | DAY | SEV | DAY |
| 3. Difficulty concentrating because of worry | ___ | Y N | ___ | Y N |
| 4. Fear that something awful may happen | ___ | Y N | ___ | Y N |
| 5. Feeling you might lose control of yourself | ___ | Y N | ___ | Y N |
| Melancholic/Atypical features | | | | |
| 6. (Un)reactive to pleasant stimuli (e.g., does/does not feel better when something good happens) If present, indicate whether mood is: Reactive or Unreactive (circle one) | ___ | Y N | ___ | Y N |
| 7. Depression worse in the morning | ___ | Y N | ___ | Y N |
| 8. Early morning awakening (at least 2 hours before intended) | ___ | Y N | ___ | Y N |
| 9. Overly sensitive to rejection from others (must result in social/occupational impairment) | ___ | Y N | ___ | Y N |

## BIPOLAR/CYCLOTHYMIA

### I. INITIAL INQUIRY

1. **Have you ever experienced a period of several days or more when you felt unusually or excessively high or irritable? This is very different from being in a good mood or feeling the effects of a substance. What I mean is a period where you felt persistently or abnormally high or irritable, perhaps along with such things as a decreased need for sleep, racing thoughts and distractibility, and an unusual increase in the number of activities you got involved in.**

YES ____ NO ____

If YES, **When was the most recent time this occurred?**

______________________________________________

**How long did this period last?** ______________________________________________

******************************************************************************************

If YES to 1. or uncertain, continue inquiry.
Otherwise skip to **ILLNESS ANXIETY DISORDER** (p. 88).

******************************************************************************************

2a. **When did these symptoms first begin?** ______________________________________________

b. **After these symptoms began, [have/did] you experience(d) them continuously, or [have there been/were there] periods of time after the symptoms began that you were not bothered by them?** [To foster subsequent inquiry, try to begin to establish dates of onset/remission and presence of more than one discrete episodes of disturbance.]

______________________________________________

______________________________________________

### II. SYMPTOM RATINGS

CURRENT symptom ratings should be obtained for patients who report current mania symptoms only. If patient only reports past mania symptoms, initially obtain PAST symptom ratings. In these cases, CURRENT symptom ratings should be obtained after establishing a past diagnosis of Bipolar/Cyclothymia in the PAST EPISODE sections (e.g., to determine partial/full remission). If there is evidence of separate episodes, inquire about the presence of discrete episodes of disturbance (e.g., "**Since these symptoms began, have there been periods of time when you were not bothered by them?**"). For patients endorsing both current and past episodes, CURRENT symptom ratings should be obtained first and PAST ratings should be obtained after completing the CURRENT EPISODE section. Record symptoms that are present during the same one-week period and represent a noticeable change from previous functioning. For symptoms that meet the criteria for hypomania but not mania (i.e., present for 4 days but less than a week), circle the severity rating.

PAST EPISODES: Obtain symptom ratings for the first (hypo)manic episode under the PAST #1 column. If there are two past (hypo)manic episodes, rate the second episode under the PAST #2 column. If there are more than two past (hypo)manic episodes, either: (a) rate the worst episode under the PAST #2 column, if the worst episode is not the first or current episode, or (b) rate the most recent past episode under the PAST #2 column, if the worst episode is the first or current episode.

CURRENT: **Over the past week, have you experienced ______________?;**
**Have you experienced ______________ most of the day and nearly every day over the past week** (4 consecutive days for hypomania)**?**

PAST: **During that period of time in __________** (dates), **did you experience ______________ ?;**
**Did you experience ______________ most of the day and nearly every day for 1 week or more** (4 consecutive days for hypomania)**?**

SEVERITY (SEV):

0------------1------------2------------3------------4------------5------------6------------7------------8

None Mild Moderate Severe Very severe

MOST OF DAY/NEARLY EVERY DAY (DAY): Indicate Yes or No

| | CURRENT | | PAST #1 (FIRST) | | PAST #2 (SECOND/WORST) | |
|---|---|---|---|---|---|---|
| | SEV | DAY | SEV | DAY | SEV | DAY |
| 1. Irritability | ___ | Y N | ___ | Y N | ___ | Y N |
| 2. Elevated or expansive mood | ___ | Y N | ___ | Y N | ___ | Y N |
| 3. Inflated self-esteem or grandiosity | ___ | Y N | ___ | Y N | ___ | Y N |
| 4. Decreased need for sleep | ___ | Y N | ___ | Y N | ___ | Y N |
| 5. More talkative than usual or pressure to keep talking | ___ | Y N | ___ | Y N | ___ | Y N |
| 6. Flight of ideas or feeling that thoughts are racing | ___ | Y N | ___ | Y N | ___ | Y N |
| 7. Distractibility | ___ | Y N | ___ | Y N | ___ | Y N |
| 8. Increase in goal-directed activity (e.g., social, work) or agitation/restlessness (purposeless activity) | ___ | Y N | ___ | Y N | ___ | Y N |
| 9. Involvement in activities with a high potential for painful consequences (e.g., buying sprees, foolish investments, sexual indiscretions) | ___ | Y N | ___ | Y N | ___ | Y N |
| 10. Delusions or hallucinations Content: ______________________________ ______________________________ | ___ | Y N | ___ | Y N | ___ | Y N |
| 11. Thoughts of death or suicide | ___ | Y N | ___ | Y N | ___ | Y N |

If YES to 11., inquire about the extent of suicidal ideation or intent (e.g., history of prior attempts, presence/extent of current plan, access to method for carrying out plan, ability to state reasons for living):

CURRENT: ________________________________________________

PAST #1: ________________________________________________

PAST #2: ________________________________________________

*Note*: Symptoms #10 and #11 are not diagnostic criteria for mania and hypomania.

**********************************************************************************************

If no evidence of (hypo)mania symptoms,
Skip to **ILLNESS ANXIETY DISORDER** (p. 88).

**********************************************************************************************

## III. CURRENT EPISODE

If evidence of a discrete past episode, preface inquiry in this section with: **Now I want to ask you a series of questions about this current/most recent period of time when you felt [unusually high/irritable] that began roughly in** _______________ (specify dates).

1. **In what ways have these symptoms interfered with your life** (e.g., daily routine, job, social activities)?; **How much are you bothered about having these symptoms?; Have these symptoms impaired your judgment or required you to be hospitalized/supervised to prevent you from harming yourself or others?**

____________________________________________

____________________________________________

Rate interference: _______________ distress: _______________

0------------1------------2------------3------------4------------5------------6------------7------------8

None Mild Moderate Severe Very severe

2a. **When did these symptoms become a problem?** (Determine when the hypo/manic symptoms met *DSM-5* threshold; i.e., when the symptoms became sufficient in number and severity to cause clinically significant interference/distress, hospitalization, etc.)

____________________________________________

Date of Disorder Onset: _______________ Month _______________ Year

b. **Can you recall anything that might have led to this problem?** (also determine if symptoms were precipitated by antidepressant treatment such as medication, ECT, light therapy.)

YES ____ NO ____

____________________________________________

____________________________________________

c. **Were you under any type of stress during this time?**

YES ____ NO ____

**What was happening in your life at the time?**

____________________________________________

____________________________________________

d. **Were these feelings immediately preceded or followed by a period of depression?** [Place (hypo)manic episode in temporal context of any current or past episodes of depression.]

YES ____ NO ____

If YES, specify: ____________________________________________

e. If applicable, **Over the past two years, did you experience a period of two months or more when you did not feel either unusually high/irritable or down/depressed?**

YES ____ NO ____

Specify: ____________________________________________

*Note*: Consider Cyclothymic Disorder in the presence of numerous periods of hypomanic symptoms (that do not meet criteria for hypomanic episode) and numerous periods of depression (not meeting major depression) when the symptoms are present at least half the time over a 2+ year period and the patient has not been without the symptoms for more than 2 months at a time.

3. **Have you been regularly taking any types of drugs or medications during this current period of symptoms** (include drugs of abuse, medication, antidepressant treatment)**?**

YES ____ NO ____

Specify (type; amount; dates of use): ______________________________

______________________________

4. **At the time of or since these symptoms began, did you have any physical condition** (e.g., pregnancy, hyperthyroidism)**?**

YES ____ NO ____

Specify (type; date of onset/remission): ______________________________

______________________________

______________________________

5a. **Besides this current period of extremely elevated/irritable mood and accompanying symptoms, have there been other, separate periods of time before this when you had these symptoms** [inquire about discrete, previous episodes of (hypo)mania that were followed by periods of remission]**?**

YES ____ NO ____

b. If YES, **When did this/these past period(s) of symptoms occur?**

______________________________

If YES, go back to SYMPTOM RATINGS, PAST (p. 82).

If NO, skip to ILLNESS ANXIETY DISORDER (p. 88)

## IV. PAST EPISODE: FIRST EPISODE

**Now I want to ask you a series of questions about the past period(s) of elevated mood/irritability that began roughly in ______________ and ended roughly in ______________** (specify dates).

1. **In what ways did these symptoms interfere with your life** (e.g., daily routine, job, social activities)**?; How much were you bothered about having these symptoms?; Did these symptoms impair your judgment or require you to be hospitalized/supervised to prevent you from harming yourself or others?**

______________________________

______________________________

Rate interference: ______________ distress: ______________

0------------1------------2------------3------------4------------5------------6------------7------------8

None Mild Moderate Severe Very severe

2a. **During that time, when did these symptoms become a problem?** (Determine when the hypo/manic symptoms met *DSM-5* threshold; i.e., when the symptoms became sufficient in number and severity to cause clinically significant interference/distress, hospitalization, etc.)

______________________________________________

Date of Disorder Onset: ______________ Month ______________ Year

b. **Can you recall anything that might have led to this problem?** (also determine if symptoms were precipitated by antidepressant treatment such as medication, ECT, light therapy)

YES ____ NO ____

______________________________________________

______________________________________________

c. **Were you under any type of stress during this time?**

YES ____ NO ____

**What was happening in your life at the time?**

______________________________________________

______________________________________________

d. **Were these feelings immediately preceded or followed by a period of depression?** [Place (hypo)manic episode in temporal context of any current or past episodes of depression.]

YES ____ NO ____

If YES, specify: ______________________________________________

e. If applicable, **During that period, did you experience a period of two months or more when you did not feel either unusually high/irritable or down/depressed?**

YES ____ NO ____

Specify: ______________________________________________

<u>Note</u>: Consider Cyclothymic Disorder in the presence of numerous periods of hypomanic symptoms (that do not meet criteria for hypomanic episode) and numerous periods of depression (not meeting major depression) when the symptoms are present at least half the time over a 2+ year period and the patient has not been without the symptoms for more than 2 months at a time.

3. **Have you been regularly taking any types of drugs or medications during that past period of symptoms** (include drugs of abuse, medication, antidepressant treatment)**?**

YES ____ NO ____

Specify (type; amount; dates of use): ______________________________________________

______________________________________________

4. **At the time of or since the symptoms began, did you have any physical condition** (e.g., pregnancy, hyperthyroidism)**?**

YES ____ NO ____

Specify (type; date of onset/remission): ______________________________________________

5a. **When was the elevated/irritable mood and symptoms accompanying this mood no longer a problem, in that they no longer occurred persistently and they did not interfere with your life?**

Date of remission: ______________ Month ______________ Year

b. **Can you recall any reasons why these symptoms were no longer a problem for you?**

YES ____ NO ____

______________________________________________________________________

______________________________________________________________________

6a. **Prior to or after this past period when you felt unusually high/irritable, have there been other, separate periods of time that we haven't covered when you have had the same problems** [inquire about discrete, other episodes of (hypo)mania that were followed by periods of remission]**?**

YES ____ NO ____

b. If YES, **When did this/these other period(s) of symptoms occur?**

______________________________________________________________________

If YES, go back to SYMPTOM RATINGS, PAST (p. 82).

If NO, go back to SYMPTOM RATINGS to obtain CURRENT ratings (p. 82); then skip to ILLNESS ANXIETY DISORDER (p. 88).

## V. PAST EPISODE: WORST/SECOND EPISODE

**Now I want to ask you a series of questions about the past period(s) of elevated mood/irritability that began roughly in ______________ and ended roughly in ______________** (specify dates).

1. **In what ways did these symptoms interfere with your life** (e.g., daily routine, job, social activities)**?; How much were you bothered about having these symptoms?; Did these symptoms impair your judgment or require you to be hospitalized/supervised to prevent you from harming yourself or others?**

______________________________________________________________________

______________________________________________________________________

Rate interference: ______________ distress: ______________

0------------1------------2------------3------------4------------5------------6------------7------------8

None Mild Moderate Severe Very severe

2a. **During that time, when did these symptoms become a problem?** (Determine when the hypo/manic symptoms met *DSM-5* threshold; i.e., when the symptoms became sufficient in number and severity to cause clinically significant interference/distress, hospitalization, etc.)

______________________________________________________________________

Date of Disorder Onset: ______________ Month ______________ Year

b. **Can you recall anything that might have led to this problem?** (also determine if symptoms were precipitated by antidepressant treatment such as medication, ECT, light therapy.)

YES ____ NO ____

______________________________________________________________________

______________________________________________________________________

c. **Were you under any type of stress during this time?**

YES ____ NO ____

**What was happening in your life at the time?**

______________________________________________

______________________________________________

d. **Were these feelings immediately preceded or followed by a period of depression?** [Place (hypo)manic episode in temporal context of any current or past episodes of depression.]

YES ____ NO ____

If YES, specify: ______________________________________________

e. If applicable, **During that period, did you experience a period of two months or more when you did not feel either unusually high/irritable or down/depressed?**

YES ____ NO ____

Specify: ______________________________________________

*Note*: Consider Cyclothymic Disorder in the presence of numerous periods of hypomanic symptoms (that do not meet criteria for hypomanic episode) and numerous periods of depression (not meeting major depression) when the symptoms are present at least half the time over a 2+ year period and the patient has not been without the symptoms for more than 2 months at a time.

3. **Have you been regularly taking any types of drugs or medications during that past period of symptoms** (include drugs of abuse, medication, antidepressant treatment)**?**

YES ____ NO ____

Specify (type; amount; dates of use): ______________________________________________

______________________________________________

4. **At the time of or since the symptoms began, did you have any physical condition** (e.g., pregnancy, hyperthyroidism)**?**

YES ____ NO ____

Specify (type; date of onset/remission): ______________________________________________

5a. **When was the elevated/irritable mood and symptoms accompanying this mood no longer a problem, in that they no longer occurred persistently and they did not interfere with your life?**

Date of remission: ______________ Month ______________ Year

b. **Can you recall any reasons why these symptoms were no longer a problem for you?**

YES ____ NO ____

______________________________________________

______________________________________________

6a. **Prior to or after this past period when you felt unusually high/irritable, have there been other, separate periods of time that we haven't covered when you have had the same problems** [inquire about discrete, other episodes of (hypo)mania that were followed by periods of remission]**?**

YES ____ NO ____

b. If YES, **When did this/these other period(s) of symptoms occur?**

______________________________________________

If YES, consider rating additional past episodes (go back to SYMPTOM RATINGS, PAST, p. 82).

If NO, go back to SYMPTOM RATINGS to obtain CURRENT ratings (p. 82); then skip to ILLNESS ANXIETY DISORDER (p. 88).

# ILLNESS ANXIETY DISORDER

## I. INITIAL INQUIRY

1a. **Over the last several months, have you continually feared or believed that you might have, or that you might contract, a serious physical disease or illness** (e.g., cancer, heart disease, AIDS)?

YES ____ NO ____

If NO, skip to 1b.

**What types of diseases/illnesses do you fear you might have or might get in the future?**

______________________________________________

______________________________________________

Skip to 2a.

b. **Have you ever experienced a period of several months when you continually feared or believed that you might have, or that you might contract, a serious physical disease or illness?**

YES ____ NO ____

If YES, **What types of diseases/illnesses did you fear you might have or might come down with?**

______________________________________________

______________________________________________

*****************************************************************************************************

If YES to either 1a. or 1b., or uncertain, continue inquiry.
Otherwise, skip to **SOMATIC SYMPTOM DISORDER** (p. 94).

*****************************************************************************************************

2a. **When did these concerns first begin?** ______________________________________________

b. **After these concerns began, [have/did] you experience(d) them continuously, or [have there been/were there] periods of time after the concerns began that you were not bothered by them?** [To foster subsequent inquiry, try to begin to establish dates of onset/remission and presence of more than one discrete episodes of disturbance.]

______________________________________________

______________________________________________

## II. CURRENT EPISODE

If evidence of a discrete past episode, preface inquiry in this section with: **Now I want to ask you a series of questions about this current period of time when you worried you have/will contract a serious disease or illness, that began roughly in** ______________ (specify dates).

List diseases/illnesses of inquiry: ______________________________________________

1a. **Do you experience certain bodily symptoms or sensations that are associated with your fear or belief that you [might have/may get]** ______________ (specify disease/illness)?

YES ____ NO ____

If YES,

b. **What symptoms do you experience?**

______________________________________________

c. **How often do these symptoms occur?**

______________________________________________

2a. **Do you have, or have you had, another medical condition that is associated with your fear or belief that you [might have/may get]** ______________ (specify disease/illness)**?**

YES ____ NO ____

Specify: ______________________________________________

______________________________________________

b. **Is there a family history of illness, or other risk factors that you are aware of, associated with your fear or belief that you [might have/may get]** ______________ (specify disease/illness)**?**

YES ____ NO ____

Specify: ______________________________________________

______________________________________________

3. **To what extent do these health concerns cause you to feel anxious on a day-to-day basis?; Do you get anxious when you learn about someone else who has fell ill or when you see health-related stories in the news, magazines, internet, etc.?**

______________________________________________

______________________________________________

Rate anxiety/distress: __________

0------------1------------2------------3------------4------------5------------6------------7------------8

None Mild Moderate Severe Very severe

4a. **Are there any actions you perform regularly to check to see whether you have developed a disease or illness** (e.g., checking body for signs of illness, seeking out information about condition)**?**

YES ____ NO ____

Specify: ______________________________________________

______________________________________________

b. **Are there any actions you take, or situations/activities you avoid, to try to reduce your concerns about having/getting** ____________ (e.g., reassurance seeking, avoiding routine medical exams, avoiding potential contact with individuals who are sick)**?**

YES ____ NO ____

Specify: ______________________________________________

______________________________________________

5a. **Have you seen a doctor, or undergone medical testing, to determine whether you have _____________ or any other physical illness?**

YES ____ NO ____

If YES,

b. **After your concerns about having/getting ______________ began, how many times have you seen a doctor and/or undergone medical tests for this condition?**

______________________________________________________________________________

c. **What have been the findings of these evaluations?**

______________________________________________________________________________

d. **If the doctor tells you s/he can find nothing wrong, do you feel reassured that you do not have a physical disease/illness?**

YES ____ NO ____

______________________________________________________________________________

6a. **Currently, how strongly do you believe that you [have/will get]** ______________ (0–100 scale where 0 = not at all and 100 = completely)?

________ %

b. **Is there any evidence you can think of that might indicate to you that you [do not have/will not get] ______________?**

YES ____ NO ____

______________________________________________________________________________

______________________________________________________________________________

7a. **When did your concerns about having/getting _________ become a problem?** (Determine when the Illness Anxiety Disorder met *DSM-5* threshold; i.e., when the preoccupation with having/acquiring a serious illness met clinical threshold.)

______________________________________________________________________________

Date of Disorder Onset: ______________ Month ______________ Year

b. **Can you recall anything that might have led to this problem?**

YES ____ NO ____

______________________________________________________________________________

______________________________________________________________________________

c. **During this time, have you been only worried about having/getting ________, or have you also been concerned about having/getting other diseases or illnesses?**

YES ____ NO ____

Specify: ______________________________________________________________________

______________________________________________________________________________

8a. **Besides this current period of concerns about your health, have there been other, separate periods of time before this when you had persistent concerns about having or getting a serious illness or disease** (inquire about discrete, previous episodes of Illness Anxiety Disorder that were followed by periods of remission)**?**

YES ____ NO ____

b. If YES, **When did this/these past period(s) of health concerns occur?**

______________________________________________________________

If YES, go to INITIAL INQUIRY/PAST EPISODE (pp. 88, 91).

If NO, skip to SOMATIC SYMPTOM DISORDER (p. 94).

## III. PAST EPISODE

**Now I want to ask you a series of questions about the past period of time when you worried you had/would contract a serious disease or illness, that began roughly in ______________** (specify dates).

List diseases/illnesses of inquiry: ______________________________________________

1a. **Did you experience certain bodily symptoms or sensations that were associated with your fear or belief that you might have had/gotten ______________** (specify disease/illness)**?**

YES ____ NO ____

If YES,

b. **What symptoms did you experience?**

______________________________________________________________

c. **How often did these symptoms occur?**

______________________________________________________________

2a. **Did you have another medical condition, either at the time of these concerns or before, that was associated with your fear or belief that you might have had/gotten ______________** (specify disease/illness)**?**

YES ____ NO ____

Specify: ______________________________________________________

______________________________________________________________

b. **Was there a family history of illness, or other risk factors that you were aware of, associated with your fear or belief that you might have had/gotten ______________** (specify disease/illness)**?**

YES ____ NO ____

Specify: ______________________________________________________

______________________________________________________________

3. **To what extent did these health concerns cause you to feel anxious on a day-to-day basis?; Did you get anxious when you learned about someone else who fell ill or when you saw health-related stories in the news, magazines, internet, etc.?**

________________________________________________________________________

________________________________________________________________________

Rate anxiety/distress: _______________

0------------1------------2------------3------------4------------5------------6------------7------------8

None Mild Moderate Severe Very severe

4a. **Were there any actions you performed regularly to check to see whether you developed a disease or illness** (e.g., checking body for signs of illness, seeking out information about condition)?

YES ____ NO ____

Specify: ______________________________________________________________

________________________________________________________________________

b. **Were there any actions you took, or situations/activities you avoided, to try to reduce your concerns about having/getting ______________** (e.g., reassurance seeking, avoiding routine medical exams, avoiding potential contact with individuals who are sick)?

YES ____ NO ____

Specify: ______________________________________________________________

________________________________________________________________________

5a. **Did you see a doctor, or undergo medical testing, to determine whether you had ________________ or any other physical illness?**

YES ____ NO ____

If YES,

b. **After your concerns about having/getting ________________ began, how many times did you see a doctor and/or undergo medical tests for this condition?**

________________________________________________________________________

c. **What were the findings of these evaluations?**

________________________________________________________________________

d. **If the doctor told you s/he found nothing wrong, did you feel reassured that you did not have a physical disease/illness?**

YES ____ NO ____

If YES, **How long did this reassurance last?** ________________________________________________________

6a. **During that time, how strongly did you believe that you [had/would get] ________________** (0–100 scale where 0 = not at all and 100 = completely)?

________ %

b. **Did you consider any contradictory evidence that indicated to you that you [did not have/would not get] ________________?**

YES ____ NO ____

If YES, have patient specify: ________________________________________________________

________________________________________________________________________

7a. **When did your concerns about having/getting __________ become a problem?** (Determine when the Illness Anxiety Disorder met *DSM-5* threshold; i.e., when the preoccupation with having/acquiring a serious illness met clinical threshold.)

________________________________________________________________________

Date of Disorder Onset: _______________ Month _______________ Year

b. **Can you recall anything that might have led to this problem?**

YES ____ NO ____

________________________________________________________________________

________________________________________________________________________

c. **During this time, were you only worried about having/getting ________, or were you also concerned about having/getting other diseases or illnesses?**

YES ____ NO ____

Specify: ________________________________________________________________

________________________________________________________________________

8a. **When did this stop being a problem for you, in that you were no longer preoccupied with having/getting _______________, and the notion of having/getting _______________ did not cause you to feel anxious or prompt you to engage in health-related actions** (e.g., self or doctor exams, maladaptive avoidance)?

Date of remission: _______________ Month _______________ Year

b. **Can you recall any reasons why these health concerns were no longer a problem for you?**

YES ____ NO ____

________________________________________________________________________

________________________________________________________________________

9a. **Prior to or after this past period of concerns about your health, have there been other, separate periods of time we haven't covered when you had persistent concerns about having or getting a serious illness or disease** (inquire about discrete, other episodes of Illness Anxiety Disorder that were followed by periods of remission)?

YES ____ NO ____

b. If YES, **When did this/these other period(s) of health concerns occur?**

________________________________________________________________________

If YES, go back to INITIAL INQUIRY (p. 88).

If NO, skip to SOMATIC SYMPTOM DISORDER (p. 94).

## SOMATIC SYMPTOM DISORDER

### I. INITIAL INQUIRY

1a. **Currently, have you been experiencing one or more physical problems or physical symptoms that have caused you significant distress or impairment in your daily life** (e.g., pain/headache, GI problems/nausea, dizziness, chronic fatigue)**?**

YES ____ NO ____

If NO, skip to 1b.

IF YES, specify: ______________________________________________

______________________________________________

Rate severity of physical symptoms: _________

0-----------1-----------2-----------3-----------4-----------5-----------6-----------7-----------8

None Mild Moderate Severe Very severe

Skip to 2a.

b. **Have you <u>ever</u> experienced a period of time when you experienced one or more physical problems or physical symptoms that caused you significant distress or impairment in your daily life** (e.g., pain/headache, GI problems/nausea, dizziness, chronic fatigue)**?**

YES ____ NO ____

IF YES, specify: ______________________________________________

______________________________________________

Rate severity of physical symptoms: _________

0-----------1-----------2-----------3-----------4-----------5-----------6-----------7-----------8

None Mild Moderate Severe Very severe

**********************************************************************************

If YES to 1a. or 1b., or uncertain, continue inquiry.

Otherwise, skip to **ALCOHOL USE DISORDER** (p. 100).

**********************************************************************************

2a. **When did these problem(s) first begin?** ______________________________________________

b. **After these problem(s) began, [have/did] you experience(d) them continuously, or [have there been/were there] periods of time after the problem(s) began that you were not bothered by them?** [To foster subsequent inquiry, try to begin to establish dates of onset/remission and presence of more than one discrete episodes of disturbance.]

______________________________________________

______________________________________________

## II. CURRENT EPISODE

If evidence of a discrete past episode, preface inquiry in this section with: **Now I want to ask you a series of questions about this <u>current</u> period of time when you experienced these physical problems/symptoms, that began roughly in _______________** (specify dates).

List physical symptoms/problems of inquiry: ________________________________________

1. **To what extent are these physical/symptoms/health concerns associated with the following...** (if present, specify nature of the symptom in the space provided and rate its severity, SEV)?

0------------1------------2------------3------------4------------5------------6------------7------------8
None Mild Moderate Severe Very severe

SEV

a. **Ongoing worries about how serious the physical symptoms/problems might be?**

__________________________________________________________ ___

b. **Daily anxiety about your health and the physical symptoms/problems?**

__________________________________________________________ ___

c. **Spending considerable time/energy trying to learn the causes and treatment for these symptoms/problems?**

__________________________________________________________ ___

2a. **Do you have, or have you had, another medical condition that you believe may be associated with your current physical symptoms/problems?**

YES ____ NO ____

Specify: ____________________________________________________________

____________________________________________________________________

b. **Is there a family history of illness, or other risk factors you are aware of, that you believe may be associated with your current physical symptoms/problems?**

YES ____ NO ____

Specify: ____________________________________________________________

____________________________________________________________________

3a. **In what ways have these physical problems/symptoms interfered with your life** (e.g., job, social activities, depletion of finances due to numerous doctor visits)?; **How much have you been bothered by these problems/symptoms?**

____________________________________________________________________

____________________________________________________________________

Rate interference: _______________ distress: _______________

0------------1------------2------------3------------4------------5------------6------------7------------8
None Mild Moderate Severe Very severe

b. **Have these physical problems/symptoms prompted you to see the doctor on several occasions?**

YES ____ NO ____

If NO, skip to 4a.

IF YES, specify: ____________________________________________

____________________________________________

c. **Have doctors had difficulty either diagnosing the source of these problems/symptoms or treating them effectively?**

YES ____ NO ____

IF YES, specify: ____________________________________________

____________________________________________

4a. **Currently, how strongly do you believe these symptoms are serious or reflect a serious problem that doctors have failed to adequately diagnose and treat** ______________ (0–100 scale where 0 = not at all and 100 = completely)**?**

________ %

b. **Is there any evidence you can think of that might indicate to you that the symptoms are not serious and may not reflect a significant medical problem?**

YES ____ NO ____

If YES, have patient specify: ____________________________________________

____________________________________________

5a. **When did these physical symptoms become a problem?** (Determine when the Somatic Symptom Disorder met *DSM-5* threshold; i.e., when the symptoms became associated with persistent and clinically significant distress and lifestyle disruption.)

____________________________________________

Date of Disorder Onset: ______________ Month ______________ Year

b. **Can you recall anything that might have led to this problem?**

YES ____ NO ____

____________________________________________

____________________________________________

c. **During this time, have the same symptoms been present consistently or have you also experienced other symptoms instead of, or in addition to, these symptoms?**

YES ____ NO ____

Specify: ____________________________________________

____________________________________________

6a. **Besides this current period of symptoms, have there been other, separate periods of time before this when you experienced these or other physical symptoms/problems persistently** (inquire about discrete, previous episodes of Somatic Symptom Disorder that were followed by periods of remission)**?**

YES ____ NO ____

b. If YES, **When did this/these past period(s) of physical symptoms/problems occur?**

______________________________________________

If YES, go to PAST EPISODE (p. 97).

If NO, skip to ALCOHOL USE DISORDER (p. 100).

## III. PAST EPISODE

If evidence of a discrete past episode, preface inquiry in this section with: **Now I want to ask you a series of questions about the past period of time when you experienced physical problems/symptoms, that began roughly in** ______________ (specify dates).

List physical symptoms/problems of inquiry: ______________________________

1. **To what extent were these physical/symptoms/health concerns associated with the following...** (if present, specify nature of the symptom in the space provided and rate its severity, SEV)**?**

0------------1------------2------------3------------4------------5------------6------------7------------8

None Mild Moderate Severe Very severe

SEV

a. **Ongoing worries about how serious the physical symptoms/problems might be?**

______________________________________________ ___

b. **Daily anxiety about your health and the physical symptoms/problems?**

______________________________________________ ___

c. **Spending considerable time/energy trying to learn the causes and treatment for the symptoms/problems?**

______________________________________________ ___

2a. **Did you have, or did you have previously, another medical condition that you believed may have been associated with the physical symptoms/problems you were experiencing?**

YES ____ NO ____

Specify: ______________________________________________

______________________________________________

b. **Was there a family history of illness, or other risk factors that you were aware of, that you believed may have been associated with the physical symptoms/problems you were experiencing?**

YES ____ NO ____

Specify: ______________________________________________

______________________________________________

3a. **In what ways did these physical problems/symptoms interfere with your life** (e.g., job, social activities, depletion of finances due to numerous doctor visits)?; **How much were you bothered by these problems/symptoms?**

______________________________________________________________________

______________________________________________________________________

Rate interference: ______________ distress: ______________

0------------1------------2------------3------------4------------5------------6------------7------------8

None Mild Moderate Severe Very severe

b. **Did these physical problems/symptoms prompt you to see the doctor on several occasions?**

YES ____ NO ____

If NO, skip to 4a.

IF YES, specify: ______________________________________________________

______________________________________________________________________

c. **Did doctors have difficulty either diagnosing the source of these problems/symptoms or treating them effectively?**

YES ____ NO ____

IF YES, specify: ______________________________________________________

______________________________________________________________________

4a. **During that time, how strongly did you believe the symptoms were serious or reflected a serious problem that doctors failed to adequately diagnose and treat** ______________ (0–100 scale where 0 = not at all and 100 = completely)?

________ %

b. **Did you consider any contradictory evidence that indicated to you that the symptoms were not serious and may not have reflected a significant medical problem?**

YES ____ NO ____

If YES, have patient specify: __________________________________________

______________________________________________________________________

5a. **When did these physical symptoms become a problem?** (Determine when the Somatic Symptom Disorder met *DSM-5* threshold; i.e., when the symptoms became associated with persistent and clinically significant distress and lifestyle disruption.)

______________________________________________________________________

Date of Disorder Onset: ______________ Month ______________ Year

b. **Can you recall anything that might have led to this problem?**

YES ____ NO ____

______________________________________________________________________

______________________________________________________________________

c. **During this time, were the same symptoms present consistently or did you also experience other symptoms instead of, or in addition to, these symptoms?**

YES ____ NO ____

Specify: ____________________________________________________________

____________________________________________________________

6a. **When did this stop being a problem for you, in that the physical symptoms/problems were no longer present or they no longer distressed you or interfered with your life?**

Date of remission: ______________ Month ______________ Year

b. **Can you recall any reasons why these physical symptoms/problems were no longer a problem for you?**

YES ____ NO ____

____________________________________________________________

____________________________________________________________

7a. **Prior to or after this past period of physical symptoms/problems, have there been other, separate periods of time we haven't covered when you experienced these or other physical symptoms/problems persistently** (inquire about discrete, other episodes of Somatic Symptom Disorder that were followed by periods of remission)?

YES ____ NO ____

b. If YES, **When did this/these other period(s) of physical symptoms/problems occur?**

____________________________________________________________

If YES, go to INITIAL INQUIRY (p. 94).

If NO, skip to ALCOHOL USE DISORDER (p. 100).

## ALCOHOL USE DISORDER

### I. INITIAL INQUIRY

1a. **Currently, how much alcohol do you typically drink?** (Specify number, type, and amount of alcoholic beverage used and indicate time period/number of drinks per occasion; e.g., "three 12 oz. beers per week.")

______________________________________________

______________________________________________

If evidence of excessive alcohol use, skip to 2a.

If no evidence of current excessive alcohol use, ask:

b. **Was there a period of time in the past when you drank considerably more than you do now?**

YES ____ NO ____

If YES,

**How much alcohol did you typically drink?** (Specify number, type, and amount of alcoholic beverage used and indicate time period/number of drinks per occasion; e.g., "three 12 oz. beers per week.")

______________________________________________

______________________________________________

**********************************************************************************************

If evidence of current or past problematic alcohol use, or uncertain, continue inquiry;
Otherwise, skip to **SUBSTANCE USE DISORDERS** (p. 104).

**********************************************************************************************

2a. **When did this level of drinking first begin?** ______________________________________________

b. **After your drinking began, [have you drank/did you drink] at roughly this same level, or [have there been/were there] periods of time after you began drinking when you drank considerably less or not at all?** [To foster subsequent inquiry, try to begin to establish dates of onset/remission and presence of more than one discrete episodes of disturbance.]

______________________________________________

______________________________________________

### II. SYMPTOM RATINGS

CURRENT symptom ratings should be obtained for patients who report current alcohol use only. If patient only reports past alcohol use, initially obtain PAST symptom ratings. In these cases, CURRENT symptom ratings should be obtained after establishing a past diagnosis of Alcohol Use Disorder in the PAST EPISODE section (e.g., to determine partial/full remission). If there is evidence of <u>separate</u> episodes, inquire about the presence of <u>discrete</u> episodes of disturbance (e.g., "**Since these symptoms began, have there been periods of time when you were not bothered by them?**"). For patients endorsing both current and past episodes, CURRENT symptom ratings should be obtained first and PAST ratings should be obtained after completing the CURRENT EPISODE section.

Rate the frequency/severity of each symptom using the scale below. If the symptom is present, provide further information as necessary.

0------------1------------2------------3------------4------------5------------6------------7------------8

| Never/ None | Rarely/Mild | Occasionally/ Moderate | Frequently/ Severe | Constantly/ Very Severe |
|---|---|---|---|---|

CURRENT: **During the past year, has your drinking been associated with the following:**

PAST: **During that time in _____** (specify dates), **was your drinking associated with the following:**

| | CURRENT | PAST |
|---|---|---|
| 1. **Drank larger amounts or over longer periods of time than you intended to?** ____________ | ____ | ____ |
| 2. **Had an ongoing desire, or found it difficult, to cut down or control your drinking?** ____________ | ____ | ____ |
| 3. **Spent a great deal of time obtaining or using alcohol or recovering from its effects?** ____________ | ____ | ____ |
| 4. **Felt a strong desire or urge to use alcohol** (craving)**?** ____________ | ____ | ____ |
| 5. **Interfered with your ability to fulfill your obligations at work, school, or home?** ____________ | ____ | ____ |
| 6. **Caused or worsened interpersonal problems with family, social, or work relationships?** ____________ | ____ | ____ |
| 7. **Gave up or cut back on work, leisure activities, or social relationships because of the alcohol?** ____________ | ____ | ____ |
| 8. **Drank in situations in which it was physically hazardous** (e.g., driving, against medical advice)**?** ____________ | ____ | ____ |
| 9. **Continued to drink while knowing you had a medical or emotional problem that the alcohol was creating or making worse?** ____________ | ____ | ____ |
| 10. Tolerance (either a. or b.) | | |
| a. **Need to drink a lot more to become intoxicated or achieve the effect you desired?** ____________ | ____ | ____ |
| b. **Notable decrease in effects of drinking the same amount of alcohol?** ____________ | ____ | ____ |
| 11. Withdrawal (either a. or b.) | | |
| a. **Unpleasant symptoms when you stopped drinking for awhile: sweating/ increased heart rate, tremor, sleep difficulties, stomach distress, hallucinations, agitation, anxiety, seizures** (two or more)**?** ____________ | ____ | ____ |
| b. **Drank or used another substance (e.g., anti-anxiety medication) to reduce or avoid alcohol withdrawal symptoms?** ____________ | ____ | ____ |

********************************************************************************************

If no evidence of current and past clinically significant alcohol use symptoms,
Skip to **SUBSTANCE USE DISORDERS** (p. 104).

********************************************************************************************

## III. CURRENT EPISODE

1. **In what ways has your drinking interfered with your life** (e.g., daily routine, job, social activities)?; **How much are you bothered by your drinking?**

______________________________________________________________________

______________________________________________________________________

Rate interference: _______________ distress: _______________

0------------1------------2------------3------------4------------5------------6------------7------------8
None Mild Moderate Severe Very severe

2a. **When did your drinking become a problem?** (Determine when the Alcohol Use Disorder met *DSM-5* threshold; i.e., when the drinking led to clinically significant impairment and distress.)

______________________________________________________________________

Date of Disorder Onset: _______________ Month _______________ Year

b. **Can you recall anything that might have led to this problem?**

YES ____ NO ____

______________________________________________________________________

______________________________________________________________________

c. **Were you under any type of stress during this time?**

YES ____ NO ____

**What was happening in your life at the time?**

______________________________________________________________________

______________________________________________________________________

3a. **Besides this current period, have there been other, separate periods of time before this when you had problems with drinking** (inquire about discrete, previous episodes of Alcohol Use Disorder that were followed by periods of remission)**?**

YES ____ NO ____

b. If YES, **When did this/these past period(s) of drinking occur?**

______________________________________________________________________

If YES, go back to SYMPTOM RATINGS, PAST (p. 101).

If NO, skip to SUBSTANCE USE DISORDERS (p. 104).

## IV. PAST EPISODE

**Now I want to ask you a series of questions about the past period of drinking that began roughly in _______________ and ended roughly in _______________** (specify dates).

1. **In what ways did your drinking interfere with your life** (e.g., daily routine, job, social activities)?**; How much were you bothered by your drinking?**

______________________________________________

______________________________________________

Rate interference: ______________ distress: ______________

0------------1------------2------------3------------4------------5------------6------------7------------8

None Mild Moderate Severe Very severe

2a. **During that time, when did your drinking become a problem?** (Determine when the Alcohol Use Disorder met *DSM-5* threshold; i.e., when the drinking led to clinically significant impairment and distress.)

______________________________________________

Date of Disorder Onset: ______________ Month ______________ Year

b. **Can you recall anything that might have led to this problem?**

YES ____ NO ____

______________________________________________

______________________________________________

c. **Were you under any type of stress during this time?**

YES ____ NO ____

**What was happening in your life at the time?**

______________________________________________

______________________________________________

3a. **When was the drinking no longer a problem, in that you were able to stop drinking or you were able to cut back or control your drinking to an extent that it no longer resulted in any of the difficulties we just talked about?**

Date of remission: ______________ Month ______________ Year

b. **Can you recall any reasons why your alcohol use was no longer a problem for you?**

YES ____ NO ____

______________________________________________

______________________________________________

4a. **Prior to or after this past period of drinking, have there been other, separate periods of time that we haven't covered when you had problems with drinking** (inquire about discrete, other episodes of Alcohol Use Disorder that were followed by periods of remission)**?**

YES ____ NO ____

b. If YES, **When did this/these other period(s) of drinking occur?**

______________________________________________

If YES, go back to SYMPTOM RATINGS, PAST (p. 101).

If NO, go back to SYMPTOM RATINGS to obtain CURRENT ratings (p. 101); then skip to SUBSTANCE USE DISORDERS (p. 104).

# SUBSTANCE USE DISORDERS

## I. INITIAL INQUIRY

1. Current and Past Substance Use

CURRENT: **In the past year, have you used/taken ______________?; How often?**
PAST: **Have you ever used/taken ______________ ?; How often?; Over what time period?**

| | CURRENT | PAST |
|---|---|---|
| a. Marijuana, hashish ________ | Y N | Y N |
| b. Cocaine ________ | Y N | Y N |
| c. Amphetamines/stimulants (e.g., "ice," ADHD drugs) ________ | Y N | Y N |
| d. Hallucinogens (e.g., LSD, PCP, ecstasy) ________ | Y N | Y N |
| e. Inhalants (e.g., glue, fuel, paint, alcohol) ________ | Y N | Y N |
| f. Opioids (e.g., heroin, analgesic opioids) ________ | Y N | Y N |
| g. Sedatives (e.g., barbiturates) ________ | Y N | Y N |
| h. Anxiolytics (e.g., benzodiazepines) ________ | Y N | Y N |
| i. Hypnotics (e.g., sleep medications) ________ | Y N | Y N |
| j. Tobacco ________ | Y N | Y N |
| k. Other: ________ ________ | Y N | Y N |

CURRENT: For each substance currently endorsed, ask the following:

**Currently, how much** _______ (specify substance) **do you typically use?** (Specify type, amount, and administration method of substance used and indicate time period/amount used per occasion; e.g., "three joints per night.")

________________________________________
________________________________________
________________________________________
________________________________________

PAST: For each substance endorsed in the past, ask the following:

**How much** ________ (specify substance) **did you typically use?** (Specify type, amount, and administration method of substance used and indicate time period/amount used per occasion; e.g., "three joints per night.")

________________________________________
________________________________________
________________________________________
________________________________________

**********************************************************************************************

If evidence of current or past problematic substance use, or uncertain, continue inquiry;
Otherwise, skip to **OTHER DISORDERS SCREENING** (p. 110).

**********************************************************************************************

2a. **When did this level of use first begin?** ______________________________________________

b. **After you began using** ______ (specify substance), **[have you used/did you use] this substance at roughly this same level, or [have there been/were there] periods of time after you began using** ______ (specify substance) **when you used it considerably less or not at all?** [To foster subsequent inquiry, try to begin to establish dates of onset/remission and presence of more than one discrete episodes of disturbance.]

__________________________________________________________________________________

__________________________________________________________________________________

__________________________________________________________________________________

__________________________________________________________________________________

## II. SYMPTOM RATINGS

CURRENT symptom ratings should be obtained for patients who report current substance use only. If patient only reports past substance use, initially obtain PAST symptom ratings. In these cases, CURRENT symptom ratings should be obtained after establishing a past diagnosis of Substance Use Disorder in the PAST EPISODES section (e.g., to determine partial/full remission). If there is evidence of <u>separate</u> episodes, inquire about the presence of <u>discrete</u> episodes of disturbance (e.g., "**Since these symptoms began, have there been periods of time when you were not bothered by them?**"). For patients endorsing both current and past episodes, CURRENT symptom ratings should be obtained first and PAST ratings should be obtained after completing the CURRENT EPISODE section.

Rate the frequency/severity of each symptom using the scale below. If the symptom is present, provide further information as necessary. Columns are provided for rating two different CURRENT and PAST substances (S1, S2).

0------------1------------2------------3------------4------------5------------6------------7------------8

| 0 | 2 | 4 | 6 | 8 |
|---|---|---|---|---|
| Never/ None | Rarely/Mild | Occasionally/ Moderate | Frequently/ Severe | Constantly/ Very Severe |

CURRENT PAST

Indicate substance(s) of inquiry: 1. ________________________ 1. ________________________

2. ________________________ 2. ________________________

CURRENT: **Over the past year, has your use of** ________ **been associated with the following:**

PAST: **During that time in** _____ (specify dates), **was your use of** ________ **associated with the following:**

| | CURRENT S1 | CURRENT S2 | PAST S1 | PAST S2 |
|---|---|---|---|---|
| 1. **Used larger amounts of** ______ **or over longer periods of time than you intended to?** ____________________ ____________________ | ___ | ___ | ___ | ___ |
| 2. **Had an ongoing desire, or found it difficult, to cut down or control your use?** ____________________ ____________________ | ___ | ___ | ___ | ___ |

0------------1------------2------------3------------4------------5------------6------------7------------8

| Never/ None | Rarely/Mild | Occasionally/ Moderate | Frequently/ Severe | Constantly/ Very Severe |
|---|---|---|---|---|

| | CURRENT S1 | CURRENT S2 | PAST S1 | PAST S2 |
|---|---|---|---|---|
| 3. **Spent a great deal of time obtaining or using ______ or recovering from its effects?** | ____ | ____ | ____ | ____ |
| 4. **Felt a strong desire or urge to use ______** (craving)? | ____ | ____ | ____ | ____ |
| 5. **Interfered with your ability to fulfill your obligations at work, school, or home?** | ____ | ____ | ____ | ____ |
| 6. **Caused or worsened interpersonal problems with family, social, or work relationships?** | ____ | ____ | ____ | ____ |
| 7. **Gave up or cut back on work, leisure activities, or social relationships because of using ______?** | ____ | ____ | ____ | ____ |
| 8. **Used ______ in situations in which it was physically hazardous** (e.g., driving, against medical advice)? | ____ | ____ | ____ | ____ |
| 9. **Continued to use ______ while knowing you had a medical or emotional problem that the substance was creating or making worse?** | ____ | ____ | ____ | ____ |
| 10. Tolerance (either a. or b.) | | | | |
| a. **Need to use a lot more of ______ to get high or achieve the effect you desired?** | ____ | ____ | ____ | ____ |
| b. **Notable decrease in effects of using the same amount of ______?** | ____ | ____ | ____ | ____ |
| 11. Withdrawal (either a. or b.) | | | | |
| a. **Unpleasant symptoms when you stopped using ______ for awhile: sweating/increased heart rate, tremor, sleep difficulties, stomach distress, hallucinations, agitation, anxiety, seizures** (two or more)? | ____ | ____ | ____ | ____ |

| | CURRENT | | PAST | |
|---|---|---|---|---|
| | S1 | S2 | S1 | S2 |
| b. **Used ______ or another substance to reduce or avoid withdrawal symptoms?** | ____ | ____ | ____ | ____ |

______________________________________________________________

______________________________________________________________

**************************************************************************************************

If no evidence of current and past clinically significant substance use symptoms, Skip to **OTHER DISORDERS SCREENING** (p. 110).

**************************************************************************************************

## III. CURRENT EPISODE

Indicate substances of inquiry: #1. ______________________________________________

#2: ______________________________________________

1. **In what ways has your use of _____ interfered with your life** (e.g., daily routine, job, social activities)**?; How much have you been bothered by your use of _____?**

______________________________________________________________

______________________________________________________________

______________________________________________________________

______________________________________________________________

#1: Rate interference: ______________ distress: ______________

#2: Rate interference: ______________ distress: ______________

0------------1------------2------------3------------4------------5------------6------------7------------8

None Mild Moderate Severe Very severe

2a. **When did your use of _____ become a problem?** (Determine when the Substance Use Disorder met *DSM-5* threshold; i.e., when the substance use led to clinically significant impairment and distress.)

______________________________________________________________

______________________________________________________________

#1. Date of Disorder Onset: ______________ Month ______________ Year

#2. Date of Disorder Onset: ______________ Month ______________ Year

b. **Can you recall anything that might have led to this problem?**

#1: YES ____ NO ____

#2: YES ____ NO ____

______________________________________________________________

______________________________________________________________

______________________________________________________________

______________________________________________________________

c. **Were you under any type of stress during this time?**

#1: YES ____ NO ____

#2: YES ____ NO ____

**What was happening in your life at the time?**

_______________________________________________

_______________________________________________

_______________________________________________

_______________________________________________

3a. **Besides this current period of use, have there been other, separate periods of time before this when you had problems with this or other substances** (inquire about discrete, previous episodes of Substance Use Disorder that were followed by periods of remission)?

YES ____ NO ____

b. If YES, **When did this/these past period(s) of substance use occur?**

_______________________________________________

If YES, go back to SYMPTOM RATINGS, PAST (p. 105).

If NO, skip to OTHER DISORDERS SCREENING (p. 110).

## IV. PAST EPISODES

**Now I want to ask you a series of questions about the past period of drinking that began roughly in _______________ and ended roughly in _______________** (specify dates).

Indicate substances of inquiry: #1. _______________________________________________

#2: _______________________________________________

1. **In what ways has your use of _____ interfered with your life** (e.g., daily routine, job, social activities)?; **How much are you bothered by your use of _____?**

_______________________________________________

_______________________________________________

_______________________________________________

_______________________________________________

#1: Rate interference: _______________ distress: _______________

#2: Rate interference: _______________ distress: _______________

0------------1------------2------------3------------4------------5------------6------------7------------8

None Mild Moderate Severe Very severe

2a. **When did your use of _____ become a problem?** (Determine when the Substance Use Disorder met *DSM-5* threshold; i.e., when the substance use led to clinically significant impairment and distress.)

_______________________________________________

_______________________________________________

#1. Date of Disorder Onset: _______________ Month _______________ Year

#2. Date of Disorder Onset: _______________ Month _______________ Year

b. **Can you recall anything that might have led to this problem?**

#1: YES ____ NO ____

#2: YES ____ NO ____

______________________________________________________________________

______________________________________________________________________

______________________________________________________________________

______________________________________________________________________

c. **Were you under any type of stress during this time?**

#1: YES ____ NO ____

#2: YES ____ NO ____

**What was happening in your life at the time?**

______________________________________________________________________

______________________________________________________________________

______________________________________________________________________

______________________________________________________________________

3a. **When was your use of ______ no longer a problem, in that you were able to stop using it or you were able to cut back or control your substance use to an extent that it no longer resulted in any of the difficulties we just talked about?**

#1: Date of remission: ______________ Month ______________ Year

#2: Date of remission: ______________ Month ______________ Year

b. **Can you recall any reasons why your substance use was no longer a problem for you?**

#1: YES ____ NO ____

#2: YES ____ NO ____

______________________________________________________________________

______________________________________________________________________

______________________________________________________________________

______________________________________________________________________

4a. **Prior to or after this past period of use, have there been other, separate periods of time that we haven't covered when you had problems with this or other substances** (inquire about discrete, other episodes of Substance Use Disorder that were followed by periods of remission)**?**

YES ____ NO ____

b. If YES, **When did this/these past period(s) of substance use occur?**

______________________________________________________________________

If YES, go back to SYMPTOM RATINGS, PAST (p. 105).

If NO, go back to SYMPTOM RATINGS to obtain CURRENT ratings (p. 105); then skip to OTHER DISORDERS SCREENING (p. 110).

## OTHER DISORDERS SCREENING

**Now I'd like to ask you a few questions about some types of symptoms and problems that we have not yet covered.**

Indicate whether the symptom is present currently or in the past. If the symptom is present, provide further information as necessary (e.g., nature of symptoms, dates/time periods).

**Have you ever experienced any of the following:**

| | CURRENT | PAST |
|---|---|---|
| 1. **Difficulty throwing or giving away possessions, regardless of their value?** ____________ ____________ | Y N | Y N |
| 2. **Difficulty controlling unwanted habits/behaviors such as hair pulling or skin picking?** ____________ ____________ | Y N | Y N |
| 3. **Concerns about your body weight or shape, or becoming fat?** ____________ ____________ | Y N | Y N |
| 4. **Either restricting or feeling out of control of your eating?** ____________ ____________ | Y N | Y N |
| 5. **Inability to remain on task** (e.g., reading, schoolwork, job) **due to difficulties staying focused or feeling restless/unable to sit still?** ____________ ____________ | Y N | Y N |
| 6. **As a child, refusing to speak in situations you were expected to** (e.g., school)**?** ____________ ____________ | Y N | Y N |
| 7. **Ongoing feelings of unreality or feeling detached from yourself or your thoughts, body, or actions?** ____________ ____________ | Y N | Y N |
| 8. **Thoughts about intentionally harming others?** ____________ ____________ | Y N | Y N |
| 9. **Hearing or seeing things that other people didn't notice?** ____________ ____________ | Y N | Y N |

| | CURRENT | PAST |
|---|---|---|
| 10. **Hearing voices or conversations when no one was around?** ____________________ ____________________ | Y N | Y N |
| 11. **Seeing visions that no one else saw?** ____________________ ____________________ | Y N | Y N |
| 12. **Had the feeling that something odd was going on around you, that people were doing things to test you or antagonize or hurt you so that you felt you had to be on guard constantly?** ____________________ ____________________ | Y N | Y N |

## FAMILY HISTORY OF PSYCHOLOGICAL DISORDERS

1. **Has anyone in your immediate, biological family** (e.g., mother, father, siblings) **ever been treated or hospitalized for anxiety, depression, substance use, or other such problems, or had any such problems but did not seek treatment?**

YES ____ NO ____

If YES, specify: ____________________

2. Inquire about each of the following (type of disorder, nature of treatment):

Disorder(s) Treatment(s)

a. Mother ____________________

b. Father ____________________

c. Sister(s) ____________________

d. Brother(s) ____________________

e. Maternal grandparents ____________________

f. Paternal grandparents ____________________

g. Other (e.g., aunts, uncles) ____________________

## SUMMARY

**What is the primary problem you want help with?; What is the major change you would like to make?**

**Is there anything else that we haven't covered or that we haven't addressed sufficiently?**

MENTAL STATUS

INTERVIEW BEHAVIOR

NOTES

NARRATIVE SUMMARY

Include presenting complaint, history, diagnostic impression, etc.

## CLINICIAN'S RATINGS AND DIAGNOSES

| ABSENT | MILD | MODERATE | SEVERE | VERY SEVERE |
|---|---|---|---|---|
| 0-------------1-------------2-------------3-------------4-------------5-------------6-------------7-------------8 | | | | |
| None | Slightly disturbing/ not really disabling | Definitely disturbing/ disabling | Markedly disturbing/ disabling | Very severely disturbing/ disabling |

### CURRENT *DSM-5* DIAGNOSES

| | SEVERITY RATING | DATE OF ONSET |
|---|---|---|
| PRINCIPAL DIAGNOSIS(ES) | | |
| ________________________ | ____ | ____________ |
| ________________________ | ____ | ____________ |
| ADDITIONAL DIAGNOSES | | |
| ________________________ | ____ | ____________ |
| ________________________ | ____ | ____________ |
| ________________________ | ____ | ____________ |
| ________________________ | ____ | ____________ |
| ________________________ | ____ | ____________ |
| ________________________ | ____ | ____________ |
| ________________________ | ____ | ____________ |

MEDICAL CONDITIONS: ____________________________________________

LIFE STRESSORS: ____________________________________________

OVERALL DISTRESS/IMPAIRMENT (use CSR scale): _______

### PAST *DSM-5* DIAGNOSES

| DIAGNOSES | SEVERITY RATING | DATE OF ONSET | DATE OF REMISSION |
|---|---|---|---|
| ________________________ | ____ | ____________ | ____________ |
| ________________________ | ____ | ____________ | ____________ |
| ________________________ | ____ | ____________ | ____________ |
| ________________________ | ____ | ____________ | ____________ |
| ________________________ | ____ | ____________ | ____________ |
| ________________________ | ____ | ____________ | ____________ |
| ________________________ | ____ | ____________ | ____________ |

Time: Start ______________ Stop ______________

Diagnostic confidence rating (0–100): ______________ If rating is < 70, please comment:

____________________________________________

____________________________________________

# ADIS-5 Diagnostic Timeline (DTL)

Patient Name: ______________________

Rater:

Stress: ______________ ______________ ______________ ______________ ______________

LES-Ps:

LES-Os

DOB

DATE

DIAG:

DOS: ______________ ______________ ______________ ______________ ______________
CONF #1: ______________ ______________ ______________ ______________ ______________
CONF #2: ______________ ______________ ______________ ______________ ______________

DOR: ______________ ______________ ______________ ______________ ______________
CONF #1: ______________ ______________ ______________ ______________ ______________
CONF #2: ______________ ______________ ______________ ______________ ______________

Confidence : 0 = not at all confident; 100 = definitely
Rater: OS: ______________ ______________ ______________ ______________ ______________
Rater: OR: ______________ ______________ ______________ ______________ ______________